Biddy Baxter, Edward Barnes
and **Lewis Bronze**
devised and wrote the
Blue Peter Book

£3.25

Hello

1

2

3

4

5

And our 22nd Blue Peter Book is a real Box of Delights!

Do you recognise any of these photographs? They've all been in Blue Peter.

Devin Stanfield, alias Kay Harker, gave us the idea for our cover after he showed us the Box on the programme. *Our* problem has been choosing which Blue Peter delights to include – there's just not enough room for them all, but we hope you'll find some of yours in the next 74 pages.

It's been an exciting year, including the introduction of our first-ever Geordie presenter and our first acrobat. When Peter began filming for his *Duncan Dares* series, Michael Sundin joined the team – straight from playing a leading part in the feature film *Return to Oz.* You can read about how Michael turned into Tik-Tok the robot on page 18.

We've helped to solve a dastardly crime, too. When Bill & Ben, the famous TV puppets of the 1950s, were scrobbled from the BBC's Children's Programmes Diamond Jubilee Exhibition, no one thought they'd ever be seen again. But thanks to sharp-eyed Michael Cook, a member of the Blue Peter Production team, they were discovered in the nick of time in a London Sale Room. And *we* discovered the secret of their Flob-a-Dob voices.

Our Safari to Kenya was an unforgettable experience – and so was the extraordinary Calke Abbey – the house where time has stood still because generations of the Harpur-Crewe family have

There!

7

9

8

6

11

10

Turn to page 76 for the answers.

never thrown anything away! We've watched the sad demolition of one of the country's great landmarks – the historic White City Stadium – dangled mid-air 170 metres high above the Derbyshire countryside – taken part in the gruelling Royal Navy Field Gun Race – cooked a three-course meal in the middle of a muddy field in the rain – and given 300 sheep a bath! Janet's broken her pelvis – but it hasn't put her off Free Fall parachuting, and Percy Thrower's amazed the doctors and carried on gardening, despite a serious heart attack.

Throughout the year, Blue Peter viewers have continued to give us our best ideas for the programme. And congratulations to 13-year-old Andrea Lees and 6-year-old James Mack who've designed the end papers for this 22nd Book. It was hard to judge the 11,961 entries for our End Papers Competition – but in the end, we chose James' suggestion for a competition for this book and you'll find all the details on page 76. Good luck if you decide to enter!

Simon Groom.   Janet Ellis

Michael Sundin   Jack   George   Goldie

STRIVING FOR SOMETHING EXTRA!

Go-Go-Go!

The pain as the metal-bound wheel tore into my shoulder almost made me pass out.

The training, which nearly killed us before we had sight of a gun, began on a dark, freezing, January morning.

When the Blue Peter film Director, Rob Benfield, asked Peter and me if we fancied joining the Devonport team for a couple of days' training, we took a look at the video of last year's Event and thought it looked quite hard, but nothing we couldn't handle.

We didn't know the half of it. The selection tests nearly killed us before we had sight of a gun.

The event is a race between three 18-men crews who have to take their gun, in pieces, over a 1.5-metre-high wall, across a 9-metre bottomless chasm, through a narrow gap in a wall, put the gun back together again and fire three rounds.

Three naval teams from Portsmouth, Devonport and the Fleet Air Arm battle it out night after night throughout the run of the Royal Tournament every summer at Earls Court.

The training begins in early January when stomachs are full of Christmas pud, and bare hands flinch at the thought of cold steel.

Plan of the course

FIRST ACTION LINE

FINISH START

ENEMY WALL

CHASM

ENEMY RAMP

HOME RAMP

SECOND ACTION

HOME WALL

"In – in – in, Simon. Come on – move!"

As I grabbed the pulley and took off, the weight of the wheel tore into my shoulder with a searing stab of pain.

This had to be the most killing thing we'd ever attempted.

The Field Gun Run has been part of naval history for over 70 years. It grew out of the reality of the Boer War when a naval brigade put ashore and manhandled two 1-ton field guns over unrelentingly rugged country to relieve the garrison at Ladysmith. Their bravery, toughness, skill and speed in bringing the guns into action after hauling them over rock faces and across terrifying chasms, became a legend. When the war was over, a Field Gun Competition was set up as an annual event in tribute to the courage and spirit of those dedicated men.

Peter and I were soon to discover that courage and spirit are still two essential qualities for the crews of the Field Gun Event.

I failed at the weightlifting. "Simon Groom, one!" was the miserable verdict.

7

The 3-mile run didn't present many problems, especially for Marathon Man Peter, but the eight 6-metre sprints in 6 seconds began to stretch us a bit, especially with Tom, a 6′2″ tall Geordie Chief Petty Officer, who, stop-watch in hand, kept us at it without a break until we qualified.

But the weight-lifting was our Waterloo.

You have to lift a 50-kilogram weight ten times above your head, without stopping. Watching the other lads, it was obvious that there was a technique involved as well as sheer strength, but as soon as I felt the dead weight of the bar, my heart sank.

"Simon Groom – one!" was the miserable verdict. Peter did better, and with a superhuman effort, his face contorted with pain and determination, he managed 6 before dropping the bar with a clang on the floor of the gym.

We were disappointed, but Tom was encouraging.

"I'm looking for lads that are keen and eager – who'll strive to give something extra – and your willingness to have a go will make up for your lack of muscles!"

We were allocated to the "B" team, but before we started, we watched a timed run by the "A" team.

Halfway through I caught Peter's eye. We didn't speak, but the meaning was clear enough. If we'd known it was like this, we'd never have come! The video had shown the action, but the pain, the blood, and the obvious danger of losing a finger – or even your head! – as the limber gun barrels and wheels were being flung about, only hit us when we saw it for real.

Every man in the 18-strong team has a number which stands for his special job. Peter was 10, the first man to

The three-metre wooden spar swung across the chasm and hit Peter with the force of an express train.

swing across the chasm – and I was number 14, the left-hand wheel man.

To get the gun across the chasm, a massive triangle of poles has to be erected, so that Peter could swing across to the other side, followed by another huge pole which he had to stand up in a hole. Then a wire rope was flung to Peter, who fixed it to his pole, and a track to carry the equipment across the chasm was established.

It took six of us to lift the 8-cwt gun barrel on to the platform. Then back to collect the wheels…

Two of us, each with wheels weighing 60 kilograms on our shoulders, grab the pulley and swung across the chasm. I gasp with pain as the weight of the wheel grinds into my collar-bone until we hit the other side like a cannon ball. Wheels to the limber – and my thumb-nail is all but removed as the bolt is rammed home. Over the wall and my exhaustion is beginning to tell. I can't make it – my foot gets caught and I fall on my back with a sickening thud that takes my mind off the pain in my thumb and my shoulder. Off to the sick-bay for a quick examination. No bones broken, just a bruise. Yes, it will hurt badly for a week. Out you go, back to the yard. This time it's a timed run. I can't run as fast as I should, but I'm determined not to let the team down. I know what's coming now. Over to the first wall – Pete's across the chasm OK. Now the barrel. Oh – my back! Wheel on shoulder, grab the pulley. Whizz! We're there!

We slammed the wheel on to the limber, but my thumb-nail got caught between the hole and the hub.

The home run. We were exhausted, but determined not to let the team down – so we made a final effort.

Through the little hole in the wall with the big wheel. Gun barrel on – wheels on. Ready – load – fire! Bang! Bang! Bang!

A plume of smoke billowed up over the yard and then silence, broken only by the heavy breathing of 18 filthy, exhausted, blood-splattered men.

"Well done lads, you can take a break now," said Tom. "And I don't mind telling you I'm impressed by the Blue Peter lads." There was a ripple of applause from the team.

I have been on Blue Peter for seven years now, and during that time I've been lucky enough to pick up one or two awards on some glitteringly smart occasions. But that ragged round of applause from those dirty, shattered men will ring in my ears for ever. It was, quite simply, the biggest compliment we've ever been paid.

Blood spattered and absolutely whacked. Peter and I are both really proud to be in this picture.

Beaumaris, in Anglesey, is three thousand miles from Bati, in Ethiopia, but they have at least one thing in common. Thanks to the generosity of Blue Peter viewers, they both benefited from our 1984 LifeSaver Appeal. In the Welsh town, the crew of *Blue Peter II* now has a new Atlantic-21 lifeboat, and the famine relief camp that sprang up at Bati during the autumn of 1984 now has a clean, fresh water supply.

Picking just one from hundreds of worthy causes for the annual Blue Peter Appeal is the hardest decision we have to make all year. We'd known for some time that the four Blue Peter lifeboats were rapidly wearing out. They have to be in tip-top condition to meet the Royal National Lifeboat Institute's stringent tests. Although our boats had saved hundreds of lives, they were past their best. To the untrained eye they looked well maintained, but the great stresses and strains put on their inflatable

fabric by every launching were beginning to tell.

There was only one thing we could do – we had provided the boats in the first place so it was up to us to replace them.

As we were putting the finishing touches to our Appeal plans, the heart-breaking film of the tragic famine in Ethiopia was being shown every night on BBC Television *News* and *Newsround*. In no time at all, Blue Peter viewers were writing to us in their thousands asking "can't we do

something to help Ethiopia?" We desperately wanted to, but what about our lifeboats?

Then one morning, our Editor, Biddy Baxter, came in to the office with an excellent idea. "There's no reason why we can't do a *double* Appeal!", she said. "We'll have *two* commodities, *two* Totalisers, *two* depots and *two* separate targets!"

With the help of Oxfam, we quickly put together a shopping list of items badly needed in the famine regions in Ethiopia. We decided to concentrate on long-term aid, like water pumps, storage tanks, tools for digging that could make land more fertile, seeds for planting, and a thirty-two tonne lorry to help ease the transport problems in Tigre, in Northern Ethiopia.

On 12 November we launched our double LifeSaver Appeal, saying: "We've got a bigger challenge for you than ever before!" We had a gigantic map of Britain's coastline with figures depicting every one of the 434 lives saved by our four lifeboats. "Our boats really are lifesavers – it's up to us to make sure our brave crews can carry on with the job," said Simon. Janet showed a few hundred of the thousands of letters you'd sent urging us to help Ethiopia, and Michael came into the studio driving the type of lorry

LifeSavers

we wanted to provide, loaded up with all the kinds of aid we hoped the LifeSavers would help us buy.

In just a couple of days, the LifeSaver Depot at Banbury was running out of space as sackfuls of packets, parcels and envelopes of stamps – for Ethiopia – and old postcards and buttons – for the lifeboats – arrived with every delivery. The stamps were all sorted and dealt with on the spot, but the envelopes marked with "B" for boats were being put on one side. Three times a week they were collected by a Roadline lorry which ran a special shuttle service down to Poole – the RNLI headquarters. In Poole, the buttons and postcards were sorted with the expert help of our friends from Phillips, the auctioneers.

We heard from several people who owed their lives to our boats. John Rogers, from Cornwall, came up to the studio and explained how he drifted out to sea after the engine in his little boat packed up on a fishing trip. "I'm only here today because of *Blue Peter IV.* Seeing her was the best sight of my life!" he said.

The news from Ethiopia did not improve. The pictures of the starving children, with matchstick limbs and not enough strength to flick the flies away from their eyes, touched everyone's hearts. We had a live telephone link-up with Michael Buerk, the BBC Correspondent whose reports sparked off the international aid effort. He stressed the need for more of the type of help the LifeSavers were providing – long-term aid that could provide help for many years.

Late in November came the news the whole Blue Peter production team had been waiting for: Simon and film director, Alex Leger, had been given permission to go to Ethiopia with a film crew. They were gone for a week and the rest of us in London were completely out of touch with them. We had no idea where they were.

When Simon came back, his face told the story – the things he'd seen were far, far worse than he'd expected, even worse than we'd seen on television. His report was a gripping and harrowing film and contained one scene in particular that is impossible to forget. The crew met a family of people walking along the road, not knowing where they were going, with no food, and no idea where

their next meal was coming from. Simon gave them some high-energy biscuits, but the helplessness in his face when the time came to move on is a sight we'll always remember.

There were thousands of letters with ideas about how to help, ideas for fund-raising, and reports of what people had done at schools, churches, youth clubs, or with friends. The totaliser quickly neared its target of 800,000 envelopes.

Meanwhile, the lifeboats' totaliser was not going up quite as fast. We'd expected that, because we knew fewer people would have old postcards and buttons, compared to used stamps. On 3 January, 1985, the lights were

flashing on the top of the Ethiopia totaliser, but the stamps didn't stop coming in. With the extra ones, we more than trebled our target, providing many more pumps and water storage tanks than we dared hope. All of them are now in Ethiopian camps and villages, improving the quality of life there.

When this boat's engine failed, John Rogers' life was saved by Blue Peter IV. A T-shirt tied to an oar raised the alarm.

Just a month later, and only twelve weeks after we launched Blue Peter's first double Appeal, we reached the target on the Lifeboats Totaliser. Our four new lifeboats have now spent a summer patrolling their stretches of our coastline, and there are dozens of people who are very, very glad and relieved that our LifeSavers reached their Target. There is still a lot of work for the world to do in Ethiopia and across Africa to remove the curse of famine, but in Ethiopia there are a few thousand families that now have clean water, better shelter, cultivated land, seed to plant, and best of all, just a little more hope to face the future with. From them, to all the LifeSavers, "Thank You".

Thanks to the generous Freepost offer the Post Office provided, millions of parcels arrived at the LifeSaver Depot in Banbury. Simon helped the children of Deddington Primary School sort the stamps into three categories: definitives, commemoratives and foreign.

Roadline to the rescue! The haulage company ran our LifeSaver Lifeline ferrying packets of buttons and postcards from the Depot ninety-five miles to the RNLI Headquarters in Poole.

Janet helped postcard expert Duncan Chilcot separate all the rarest postcards that were sent to Poole.

Just some of the thousands of urgent requests you sent Blue Peter asking for help for the people suffering in the Ethiopian famine that started the Appeal.

After Simon's reports from Ethiopia the letters – and the used stamps pouring into Banbury – seemed to double.

Simon's Ethiopian Diary

I flew to Ethiopia on a plane packed with supplies.

The camp at Bati. ▼

DAY ONE

Up at 6 a.m., met Oxfam guide, Mikiel... filmed leaving town...
suburbs colourful with sheep, goats and cattle coming to town.
Lunch... a tablecloth-size pancake and lentils... grim loo, didn't try it!
Drove on, began seeing refugees... gave out high-energy biscuits.

DAY TWO

Drove from Dessie through mountains... beautiful scenery... eucalyptus trees... man
ploughing with oxen... hawks, eagles and storks overhead. Arrived at Bati,
20,000 people in camp... burial of child as we arrived... it's very hot and dusty,
camp ramshackle, seems chaotic, constant sound of coughing... flies, smell
overwhelming. A boy latched on to me... Mohammed Said, he stayed
with me for 3 hours... gave him my Blue Peter badge.

DAY THREE

Another amazing drive, this time to Bora... dusty, twisting road... met
Oxfam workers, ate lunch with them... filmed building of water tank, quick
and simple, will last 25 years. Intensive feeding centre – very upsetting...
desperately thin children... one boy - parents dead - looking after two
sick younger brothers. One skeletal baby with appalling diarrhoea...
no comfort in dark, over-crowded room.

DAY FOUR

Came across people sitting on a hillside... it's called a transit camp,
but nothing for them, not even from aid agencies. 1500 people,
but no food, toilets or shelter. People just <u>waiting</u>, for what...
Felt amazing spirit there... no complaining, no crime.

DAY FIVE

Back to Addis to rest, flight tomorrow. Hard to believe I'll soon be
back home, with food, shelter and warmth. The refugees will still
be at Bati, Bora and on that bleak hillside.

Mikiel introduced me to a
woman who had lost nearly all her family.

Clear spring water provided by the Appeal at Chenha, South Ethiopia.

These four nineteenth-century painted porcelain buttons with their sparkling diamante surround fetched £100 in our LifeSaver Auction.

A LifeSaver spring protection scheme at Ochollo ensures a good water supply for homes and crops.

January 3 1985, and Studio One at Television Centre is packed with long-term aid for Ethiopia and two new Lifeboats – Blue Peter I for Littlehampton and Blue Peter III for North Berwick. Well done, LifeSavers!

The men of the Grimsby lifeboat pose for the camera at the beginning of the century. Now their postcard has helped *our* lifeboats 80 years later.

STOP PRESS

By June 1985 we were well on our way to a fifth Lifeboat! And your stamps had provided **four** times our original target of long term aid for Ethiopia. We've been able to improve water supplies in Northern Ethiopia, with development and irrigation projects including water storage and distribution for the feeding centres, and also thanks to you, the LifeSaver Appeal has funded an important well digging scheme for Southern Ethiopia.

GLITTER STARS

Have a sparkling Christmas with Glitter Stars! They're cheap and easy to make and all the shapes are cut from a clear, plastic egg box – you can turn them into candle-holders and Christmas bells, too.

1 Cut off one of the egg-holding sections as deep as possible – take care the plastic doesn't split.

Trim the cut edges

Cut down the side as far as the base all the way round

Flatten out the sections

Tie a knot in a length of cotton and thread through the tip of one of the segments with a needle.

2 Remove the needle and lay the star flat on a large sheet of newspaper. Spread a thin layer of glue over it, place it on a fresh sheet of paper, and sprinkle glitter all over it.

Lift the star by the thread and shake off any spare glitter – you can use it again!

3 Wait until the glue has dried and cover the other side of the star in the same way, using different coloured glitter if you have any. Glue a scrap of tinsel in the centre.

Star Circle

Make six stars, but *without* the hanging threads.

Cut out leaf shapes from the rest of the egg box

Glue one side and cover with green glitter.

Using a saucer as a pattern, cut out a cardboard ring and cover with kitchen foil.

Glue the stars and the leaf shapes round the ring – you can hang it as a wall decoration or lay it flat for a table centrepiece.

Glitter Bells

Cut out two egg-holding sections as deep as you can and trim the cut edges. Spread glue all over the inside and the outside of each section and sprinkle on your glitter. (Silver glitter inside and gold glitter outside looks pretty!) Make a small hole at the top of the bells and thread through ribbon or Christmas parcel string, tying a knot inside each bell.

For a finishing touch, add a small bow with a scrap of tinsel.

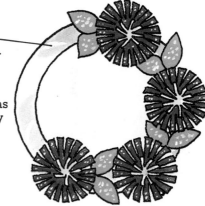

Star Candle

Fix a candle onto a tin lid using a lump of modelling clay.

Put a little fireproof tinsel round the base and put a circle of stars over it.

TRAMP

12 months old in his pram in Gateshead's
Saltwell Park.

Aged 5 and looking after his younger
brother, David.

When four-year-old Michael Sundin of Low Fell in Gateshead sat watching his
favourite programme on TV – Blue Peter – little did he think that one day he'd
be in front of the cameras himself!

"Thirteen's my lucky number," said Michael to the newspaper reporters and photographers who crowded round him when it was announced he was taking over from Peter Duncan. "I'm the programme's 13th presenter, and my very first Blue Peter appearance is on 13 September."

When I came to London, I was determined to try and persuade the Blue Peter team to give me an audition – I couldn't believe my luck when they asked me to do an interview on a trampoline – that made me feel really at home!"

16 years old and winner of Britain's Top Award for trampolining style – beating contestants of all ages and both sexes.

out of the four members of Britain's winning boys team were Sundins.

"When I was living in Low Fell and going to Breckenbeds Junior High School, I was only a few doors away from Brendan Foster – he was my idol, and I hoped I'd be as good in my field as Brendan was in his."

Trampolining led to dancing and Michael took third prize in a national disco dancing contest. He formed his own dance group, *Midnight Fantasy*, and after he left school with 9 'O' levels, he gave up his job as a computer programmer for a dancing part in panto. It was in *Jack and the Beanstalk* at Newcastle's Theatre Royal with bouncy Barbara Windsor as the star.

But Michael's big break came when he was 20 and auditioned for Andrew Lloyd Webber's musical, *Cats*. "My trampolining and dancing stood me in very good stead. I was lucky enough to be picked to play Bill Bailey, and had to perform some complicated acrobatics. Once when I was somersaulting right round the stage my wig began to slip, so I had to finish the routine with my hand holding it on to my head!

As Bill Bailey in *Cats* Michael had to perform complicated acrobatics.

No wonder. Unknown to the Blue Peter production team, Michael had a fistful of trampoline awards. He started winning titles when he was only 12 years old. In 1976, together with Blue Peter Gold Badge Winner, Carl Furrer, Michael became the World Synchro Champion in the 15- to 18-year-old age group, and went on to become a member of Britain's Men's National Squad. His younger brother, David, is a trampolinist, too, and was British champion in the under 15s group when Michael won his under 18s titles. His cousin, Ian, bounced pretty high as well – in 1972 three

Michael brought his *Cats* costume to the studio on his very first Blue Peter day.

Michael's brilliant acrobatics in *Cats* were spotted by Disney talent scouts, who signed him up for their new spectacular feature film *Return To Oz*. You can read all about Tik-Tok the Robot over the page – and that's where Blue Peter came in. We filmed behind the scenes at Elstree Studioss for Michael's very first Blue Peter film.

With 77 programmes under his belt – what next? Michael has no doubts at all. "My lifelong ambitions have been fulfilled – and with Blue Peter anything could be round the corner."

Oz

The ruins of the Emerald City - newly built at Elstree film studios!

Taking part in the big Disney film *Return to Oz* was an experience I won't forget in a hurry! My costume was only half my size and it was so excruciatingly uncomfortable, I could only stay strapped inside it for a few minutes at a time!

The film's a sequel to the famous *Wizard of Oz* that was made in Hollywood in 1939. This extraordinary adventure fantasy was all about a girl called Dorothy and her dog, Toto, and their friends the Cowardly Lion, the Tin Man and the Scarecrow, who all set off to find the Wizard.

Frank Baum, the American who wrote the story 85 years ago, followed it up with thirteen more adventures. They're all set in the Land of Oz with intruiguing titles like *The Emerald City of Oz*, *The Tik-Tok of Oz*, *The Patchwork Girl of Oz* and *The Magic of Oz*, and they're so popular in the United

Before I doubled up inside my Tik-Tok costume, I always had to do warm-up exercises like a ballet dancer to keep my body supple.

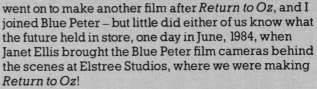

went on to make another film after *Return to Oz*, and I joined Blue Peter – but little did either of us know what the future held in store, one day in June, 1984, when Janet Ellis brought the Blue Peter film cameras behind the scenes at Elstree Studios, where we were making *Return to Oz*!

Janet met me very early in the morning – not in the make-up room, where the actors spend hours getting their faces just right for the powerful film lights, but in a small room tucked away at the back of the studios where I did my warm-up exercises. Tik-Tok is a very small, tubby robot, and to get inside the costume, I had to double up, bend down, tuck my head between my legs and cross my arms! Oh yes – and I had to walk

Getting inside was quite a performance!

States that hundreds and thousands of paperback editions are sold each year.

Frank Baum turned his first story *The Wonderful Wizard of Oz* into a stage musical. It was a huge success and ran for over eight years. There were lots of Oz films, too, but none as famous as the one made in 1939 with the leading part of Dorothy acted by Judy Garland.

In *Return to Oz*, Dorothy is played by 9-year-old Fairuza Balk, and she and I became great friends during the filming. Fairuza

Bent double, head between my legs and arms crossed, I was firmly strapped down with webbing belts before the top half of the costume was clamped over me.

backwards, as well! If I didn't warm up, like a ballet dancer, I'd get unbelievably stiff by the end of the day.

The Tik-Tok costume was in two halves – like a beach ball – with legs, arms and a head. It was designed by Lyall Conway, the Special Effects wizard who created Miss Piggy and the Skeksis, and it cost a cool quarter of a million pounds.

I wore ordinary boxing boots on my feet – inside the costume – they had self-sticking fabric on their soles so that they stuck firmly on Tik-Tok's feet and so that my leg movements were synchronised with the costumes – if I moved my toes, Tik-Tok moved his.

It was my idea for Tik-Tok to walk backwards, and I'm rather proud of that! It made him much more pompous and jerky – although it was agony at the

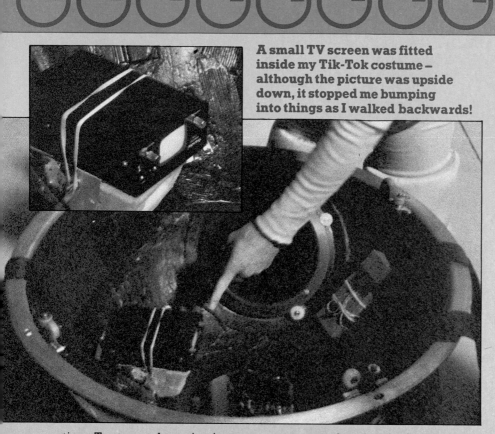

A small TV screen was fitted inside my Tik-Tok costume – although the picture was upside down, it stopped me bumping into things as I walked backwards!

time. To stop me bumping into things, there was a small TV screen inside Tik-Tok's body – it took a bit of getting used to, because the picture was upside-down – but if you're walking backwards anyway, that's the least of your problems!

After I'd been strapped inside with wide, webbing belts, the top half of the costume was clamped down – it was just as well I don't suffer from claustrophobia! Tik-Tok's face was the only part of my costume I didn't operate myself – that worked by remote control, with Tim Rose and Ian Rolph turning my head, blinking my eyes and twirling my moustache. The moustache gives Tik-Tok a suitably military flavour – he's the only survivor of the army that used to guard the Emerald City.

The Emerald City itself, with its huge tower and castles, was specially built out of plywood, plaster and polystyrene. It was all deliberately wrecked and run down, because in the story, evil forces have captured the City and let it go to rack and ruin. Janet said it felt very spooky when I showed her round the set!

On the day of Blue Peter's visit,

we were shooting the finale – the Grand Parade at the end of the film. There were so many characters, the director had to use a microphone to give us his instructions: "... Tik-Tok, Dorothy riding on the Lion, Tin Man and Scarecrow – Jack, Mombi carried

in the cage, Billina ..." he yelled as hundreds of us tried to find our places. Billina was another special effects masterpiece – a remote-controlled, radio-controlled, talking hen! Lyall said it was his most difficult challenge because she had to be totally realistic – "everyone's so familiar with the way a chicken moves – chickens have been doing it for years!"

I wasn't the only one suffering from the heat. Lots of the other costumes were unccmfortable,

The costumes for Tik-Tok and the Tin Man were based on the illustrations in Frank Baum's Oz books.

too. The Cowardly Lion, with his fur and mane woven from horsehair, was dripping with sweat. The temperature from the lights was well up into the 80s, and in between takes, giant fans were turned on to try and cool us down. I even had a little fan of my own, and my friend Fairuza used to switch it on for me whenever I was allowed a breather.

Fairuza comes from Canada, so she didn't know about Blue Peter. But Janet told her all about the programme and when they compared notes, they discovered that they both had to wear the same kind of radio microphones. Fairuza's was plugged in underneath her voluminous skirts – completely concealed – just like the ones we use on TV.

It's been a big upheaval for Fairuza, acting a leading part in a full-length feature film. She has to have ordinary lessons, of course, but on top of those and learning her lines, and all the fittings for costumes, and her make-up, there's a lot of travelling, too. When films are finally released, the leading characters fly all over the world, making public appearances and attending the different film premières.

Fairuza and I became great friends. She hadn't heard of Blue Peter in Canada, so I invited her to see our office and all our souvenirs.

The heroine of the adventure is Dorothy, played by 9-year old Fairuza Balk. We had lots of scenes together – and here, in the Hall of Mirrors, Fairuza's carrying one of our co-stars, Billina, the talking hen.

People who remember *The Wizard of Oz* are bound to compare the two Dorothys, and I think Fairuza will get lots of praise. It's not easy following in the footsteps of an actress who's become a legend, but I can't think of a better Dorothy for *Return to Oz*. As for Tik-Tok – I think once is enough. The next time anyone talks to me about the glamour of filming, I'll get them to try tying themselves in a knot with their head between their legs – walking backwards!

UNHAPPY LANDINGS

As soon as I got back from Kenya, I began training in earnest for my 25,000' free fall descent. I was well aware of the difference between the 12,000' drop I had made in the spring and "the big one", as the Falcons call it, and I also knew that practice in the air on every possible occasion was the only way I was going to make it.

When I first started free fall training at Brize Norton, my arrival used to cause something of a stir. Girls are fairly thin on the ground at the average RAF camp, and they are even thinner in the air or on the end of a parachute! But by the end of September, I was such a familiar figure I didn't rate a second glance. A friendly nod and a plain "Hello Janet" greeted me as I arrived day after day in the briefing room to find out what the flying conditions were like.

On 12 September, I rose at 6.00 am and drove out of London into the pleasant, Oxfordshire countryside. By 8.00 am I was passing through the big gates marked "RAF Brize Norton". The cloud level was pretty low and I wasn't at all surprised to see Nigel at the briefing room door pulling a wry face.

"It's no go for free falling at the moment, I'm afraid, but the met. men think the cloud might lift a bit later on." That was the worst news. The unacceptable face of free falling is the hours spent hanging around waiting for cloud to disperse. Nigel went off to supervise a ground training session whilst I slowly got into my gear and then sat down with the papers.

By 11 o'clock I was bored stiff. Nigel reappeared saying that the cloud hadn't moved – free falling was off for the day. However, an aircraft was about to take off with a party of soldiers making a static-line descent from 2500 feet – did I fancy it?

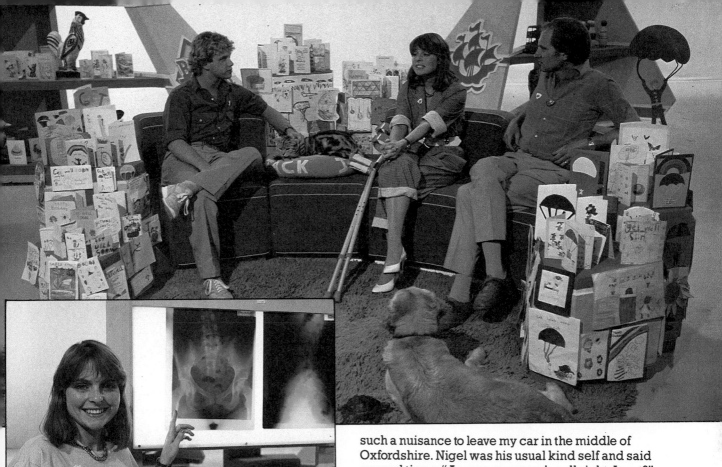

It was not a fractured femur but a broken pelvis.

It didn't sound madly thrilling as I had passed on from static-line jumping six months ago, but it was better than sitting in the briefing room, all dressed up and nowhere to go. Nigel said that at least I could practise my landings – little did he know!

I took my place in the parachute seat in the aircraft and waited for the light which told us to stand by. Most of the soldiers were jumping for the first time and looked a little tense about the eyes. It was rather nice to be the old, experienced one for a change. I joined the line, waited for the dispatcher to call go! – and jumped. Quite a good exit, I thought, as I felt the now familiar jerk and watched the parachute billow out. It was a fairly rapid descent because there was no wind, and I hit the ground with a slightly bigger thump than usual, but nothing to cause comment. I rolled over in the way I'd been taught and then began to get up to recover the parachute. But I couldn't move. My legs didn't seem to want to support me. I watched the rest of the soldiers gathering up their 'chutes and making for the lorry, but I was absolutely stuck.

After what seemed a very long time lying in the grass, Nigel came bombing round the perimeter track in his mini. "Good exit, Janet, but it looked like a hard landing. … What are you lying there for?"

Eventually Nigel got me into his car and we drove off for debriefing. By the time I got back I was still in pain, but as I could wiggle all my toes, we all decided I had pulled a muscle. I insisted on driving myself home, largely because it would have been such a nuisance to leave my car in the middle of Oxfordshire. Nigel was his usual kind self and said several times: "Are you sure you're all right, Janet?"

"I'll be OK," I reassured him and headed off down the motorway for home.

I must admit, I didn't really enjoy that drive. The pain at the base of my spine became worse with every mile, and when I got back home I just couldn't get out of the car. Help eventually arrived in the shape of my parents who took one look at me and drove me straight to the hospital.

The doctors diagnosed a hairline fracture of the femur. No operation – no plaster – just rest. The pain was pretty bad and I didn't sleep much that night.

The next day was Monday. The Blue Peter office was on the phone to the hospital. "Would I be well enough to cope with a live insert into Blue Peter?" "Yes, of course," I said.

Everyone was so kind, and the nurses and the doctors, took the turning of their ward into a television studio completely in their stride!

The following Monday I was back in the studio on crutches. The doctors decided that I had a hairline fracture of the pelvis, not the femur, which, although it sounded worse, was actually better. Two weeks later I had thrown my crutches away, and I've been as fit as a fiddle ever since. Although I wouldn't like to do it again, I shall always treasure the thousands and thousands of letters and cards you all sent to me whilst I was in hospital. It actually did hurt rather a lot at first, and if I was tempted to feel a bit sorry for myself, the warm glow of all your loving messages soon perked me up and got me back on my feet in record time.

And now, I can't wait for the spring – and getting back to Brize Norton to carry on where I left off. I hope that when you read this, I will be several stages nearer the world record for a civilian free faller!

DOLLY SHEPHERD

Dolly's knickerbocker suit was very daring for an Edwardian girl!

In those days, most people thought balloons were the nearest Man would ever get to flying. Aeronautical displays with balloons were popular at fêtes and galas all over the country, and in 1904, Captain Auguste Gaudron, an expert balloonist from France, gave spectacular programmes at Alexandra Palace, in North London, with hot-air and gas-filled balloons, and daring parachute descents actually from the balloons.

Dolly Shepherd was one of the enthusiastic onlookers. She was 17 years old and had a temporary job as a waitress in the Ally Pally refreshment room, which is how she got to know the "aeronauts" as the balloonists and parachutists were called.

One day, Captain Gaudron asked Dolly if *she* would like to make a parachute descent! And Dolly reacted just like I did – she jumped at the chance and said "Yes!" But there the resemblance between us ends. I was given weeks of rigorous training before my first jump – Dolly had just one training session and it lasted *thirty minutes!* But in that time she was taught the most important thing of all – how to fall – and told never to land in a standing position.

There was one good thing about lying in my hospital bed – I was able to catch up with my reading, and there was one book I found absolutely un-put-downable! It was called *When the 'Chute Went Up,* and it's an extraordinary account of the early days of parachuting by a girl called Dolly Shepherd, who pioneered the sport for women 80 years ago. And this was when parachute jumping was as far from respectability as a well-brought-up young lady could get!

Captain Gaudron was very fussy about her costume. Dolly left off the sweeping skirts and huge hats of a smart Edwardian young lady, and wore a peaked cap and a navy-blue knickerbocker suit with gold trimmings and high boots. Unfortunately, the boots weren't ready in time, so she had to do her first jump in ordinary shoes!

Dolly loved her parachuting outfit, particularly the boots, and said it was "very swish".

Dolly's first trip was a "Right Away" Balloon Descent. Captain Gaudron called "Hands Off" and the balloon floated skywards, with the Captain, four rather nervous passengers, and Dolly. Her silk parachute was tied with string to the balloon netting, and Dolly sat on the edge of the wicker basket, her legs dangling outside, holding on to a trapeze bar.

The spectators cheered and waved, but Dolly didn't wave back – she was too busy holding on!

All too soon, the Captain said: "Two thousand feet – ready to jump. There's a nice, green field – remember how to land – Go!"

So Dolly launched herself into space. To her relief, her weight broke the string holding the parachute to the balloon, and the jump went according to plan with the balloon sailing "Right Away".

Dolly was wildly excited. "I've done it!" she cried out, "and I want to do it all over again!" I know how she felt. *I* was wildly excited after my first jump – but I should have been terrified of using her equipment with no harness.

Dolly went on to make many more parachute descents, and became a star attraction. She was paid two pounds and ten shillings for each jump.

At last she performed the most daring feat of all – a *double* jump from a floating, unmanned balloon, with another parachutist beside her. This became the most popular of all the stunts, but one day, when Dolly was doing the double jump with a girl called Louie May, disaster struck. Louie was to jump first, but when she pulled the liberating cord – nothing happened. The release mechanism was stuck fast. She could not pull her parachute free from the balloon – she might drift for hours, clutching her trapeze bar, until the balloon came down to earth – *if* she could hold on that long!

Not for a second did Dolly think of releasing her own parachute and floating free, leaving Louie to her fate. She pulled Louie across, so that Louie

Dolly with her 'solo' balloon at Ashby. Captain Gaudron is on her right and her parachute is laid out ready to be attached to the balloon.

could clutch her neck with her arms, and Dolly's waist with her legs. Then Dolly released her own parachute and the two girls fell away together, both on a single parachute!

The double weight of the two girls affected their rate of fall and they landed heavily. Dolly was badly hurt. Like me, she damaged

25

The Illustrated Police Budget printed this picture of Dolly's mid-air rescue – not much like the real thing!

THRILLING ADVENTURE OF TWO LADY PARACHUTISTS.

Saving her partner's life when their double jump went disasterously wrong.

her pelvis, but she also injured her spine, and at first the doctors were afraid she wouldn't be able to walk again – let alone make another parachute jump. But Dolly refused to believe it. She exercised and practised, and soon she could walk a few steps. And just eight weeks after her accident she was ready to make another jump!

Dolly Shepherd was a parachute star for eight years. Then her career stopped as suddenly as it had begun – at the very same place – Alexandra Palace.

One day, when she was making a descent, she was certain she heard a voice call to her out of the empty sky: "Don't jump again!"

In the firm belief that it was the voice of God, she called back: "All right," and when she reached the ground safely, she gave her cap and badges to the surprised spectators. Then she said to Captain Gaudron: "I won't be jumping again!" – and she never did!

Dolly Shepherd died just before her 97th birthday. I'm bitterly sorry I was never lucky enough to meet her – but some people who did, are very good friends of mine – the RAF Falcons

---

1908. **LLOYD'S WEEKLY NEWS.**

HEROINES OF THRILLING PARACHUTE ADVENTURE.

Photographs of Miss Louie May (on the right) and Miss Dolly Shepard, the daring girls whose parachute adventure is related on this page. At the height of over two miles Miss May's parachute could not be released from the balloon, and she leaped a distance of several feet to Miss Shepard, who was seriously injured in the final descent.

This inaccurate account of the rescue was in the papers.

Just before her 97th birthday, Dolly met my friends, the RAF Falcons!

– including Nigel and Ally, and all the team who are training me.

Dolly finished her book just before she died. She dedicated it to "All Parachutists – Past, Present and Future."

She was certainly a great parachutist of the past, and when I read her book in hospital, I gritted my teeth and made up my mind I would be a present-day parachutist again – in the very near future!

Royal Rags

I watched a riding session on Chigwell's new outdoor arena.

It's been a Royal year for Rags, our pony for Disabled Riders. Princess Anne visited the Chigwell stables where Rags has lived since 1977 and presented her with a special Long Service Rosette. Rags certainly deserves it. Malcolm Bridson, who runs the stables, has worked out that Rags has given nearly 10,000 rides to disabled people. In all that time, she's never lost her temper, or hurt anyone, or done anything to spoil the excellent reputation of the Pony Riding for the Disabled Trust.

I met Rags a few weeks after I joined Blue Peter. Malcolm brought her along to the Garden and helped me into the saddle. I've ridden before, but I'm not experienced enough to leap into any saddle and feel at home. Rags sensed my nervousness and treated me as gently as any of the young riders she meets at Chigwell.

When I went to the stables, I saw how Malcolm and his team run the riding lessons for disabled people, with at least one, and sometimes two handlers at the head of every horse. Just a few minutes with thirteen-year-old Alison who's mentally handicapped and deaf, or with John who's suffered from polio all his adult life, show how much their weekly visit to the stables means to them. For people who cannot walk, or who have lost the use of their limbs, the freedom and sense of achievement that riding gives is obvious and a joy to see.

Malcolm has plenty to feel proud about, too. He's led a team which raised thousands of pounds to build the new arena. The all-weather surface allows severely handicapped people to ride in the fresh air. They'd only had a small, indoor hall before.

DILLnDEN

Scrobbled!

It was 25 May, 1983. The great Exhibition of 60 Years of Children's Programmes, fresh from its record-breaking triumph at the Langham Gallery in London, was on the move. The entire exhibition, every piece of it, was meticulously packed and sent off on a tour of the British Isles. The first stop was Edinburgh where the Exhibition was to be part of the Edinburgh Festival. Huge pantechnicans loaded with the history of Children's Programmes, rumbled out of London's West End and headed north.............

But when they arrived in Edinburgh one vital part of their cargo was missing. Bill and Ben – the Flower Pot Men – who had enchanted most Blue Peter viewers' fathers and mothers as they sat on *their* parents' knees, had mysteriously disappeared.

Bill and Ben were string puppets who once appeared

Peter Hawkins, the original voice of Bill and Ben, joined us in the studio to celebrate the return of the flower-pot men.

every week on their own show made for children too young to go to school.

They had a strange language:

Udo Bib = Hello Bill
Udo Bed = Hello Ben
Udo Ikl Weeb = Hello little weed
Udo Slogalog = Hello slowcoach (i.e. the tortoise)

Children all understood perfectly, but many adults were mystified and angry because they thought that their children might grow up speaking nothing but the "Bill and Ben" language.

The programme has not been on television for 20 years, but because they were so famous in their day, the original puppets are now a unique part of the BBC's history.

No wonder the whole place was thrown into a turmoil when they failed to turn up in Edinburgh. The Director-General phoned the Head of Children's Programmes who started a nationwide search. The BBC Investigators were

informed, dozens of people were questioned, and the search continued for weeks – but to no avail. Bill and Ben had disappeared from the landscape, and gradually hopes of ever seeing them again began to fade.

Two years slipped by. And then, one day, Michael Cook, a member of the Blue Peter team, was looking through some items which were going to be placed in an Auction Sale, in the hope of finding something interesting to put into the next Blue Peter programme. He was about to pack up and go home when his eyes lighted on two puppets lying abandonned in the bottom of an old bath.

It was Bill and Ben.

At first he thought they were copies, but as he examined them more closely it dawned on him that he was looking at the real thing.

The rest is history. Michael told Biddy Baxter, who told the Head of Children's Programmes, who told

The press arrived to try to get the inside story.

the Director-General. Most important of all, Freda Lingstom, the lady who had invented Bill and Ben, was told that they had been found "alive and well".

All the newspapers converged on the Blue Peter studio to take pictures of Bill and Ben, and to hear Michael's story.

But where had they been? The man who had taken the puppets to the auction rooms had bought them from an antique shop, and the antique shop owner had bought them from a stall – but neither of them knew that they were handling the real "Bill and Ben".

In the original Bill and Ben stories there was another character called little Weed, who grew between the flower pots and knew all about the mysterious Flower Pot Men, but would never reveal their secret to the gardeners. But the mystery of who scrobbled Bill and Ben remains unsolved. The BBC Investigators couldn't find out, and if little Weed knows, she certainly won't tell anyone!

WHITE CITY FAREWELL

BANG! Clank, clank, BOING!!!!!!
That's the sound of a huge concrete ball on the end of a long, steel chain being dropped again and again onto a derelict building. It was the sound and sight that met me when I walked into the famous old White City Stadium for the very last time.

The Stadium was our next-door neighbour at BBC Television Centre and for many years the two buildings were landmarks in the boring urban sprawl of West London. But the Stadium had been under threat for a long while, and eventually, in the autumn of 1984, the demolition men moved in. I went along one day to see how you go about destroying such an enormous place, and to have a final look at White City.

White City had a glorious start seventy-seven years ago. It was opened in 1908 by King Edward VII when it was the site of the Olympic Games which were held for the first time that year in London. But the Stadium was built as part of a much bigger project that opened in the same year – the Great Franco-British Exhibition.

The Exhibition was the most amazing event. There's never been anything before or since that's matched its extraordinary, lavish architecture. The idea was to show all aspects of life in Britain and France, including the genius of inventors, the wealth of trade and industry, and the vast extent of the Empires owned by each country. And once they'd feasted their eyes on all the exhibits, visitors could enjoy the thrills and spills of the enormous funfair, where amusements and rides had names like the Wiggle Woggle, the Hurly Burly, the Glacier Glide and the Cake Walk. One terrifying ride was one of the tallest structures in the whole of London. The giant arms of the Flip Flap reached sixty metres into the air to give its daredevil passengers a bird's-eye view of the Exhibition.

What they would have seen from up there explains how the Stadium got its name. All the buildings at the Exhibition were white. Marble, wood, stone or brick – they were all painted white. White walls, white roofs, white pavements, White City! To this day, the area that was once the Exhibition site is called White City. Looking back it's difficult to imagine how impressive the White City Franco-British Exhibition would have been to the millions of visitors. Those were the days before films or television and huge extravaganzas were marvellous entertainment. Perhaps the nearest equivalent today would be Disneyland and Epcot Center rolled into one, with the Los Angeles

Olympics thrown in for good measure.

The 1908 Olympic Games had little in common with the razzamatazz of the 1984 Olympics. There were far fewer sports and nearly all of them took place in the main Stadium – even the swimming. An open-air swimming pool was dug alongside the running track and the swimmers braved the cold water while they raced for their medals. Another difference was that many events were won by British athletes! But the athlete that's best remembered from those Games wasn't a winner at all, but the most

From the giant Flip Flap visitors had a fantastic view of the Exhibition site spread out before them.

At the time, it was of no importance to Pietre. He was rushed to hospital fighting for his life. Happily, he recovered and was presented with a special consolation medal, and his story has gone down in the history of athletics. It just shows how we all love a gallant loser.

◄ **The helping hands that lost the 1908 Marathon.**

World Cup football 56 years later.

famous *loser* in the history of sport.

He was a little Italian taxi-driver called Dorando Pietre, and he competed in the Marathon. A great cheer went up as he entered the Stadium first after the gruelling twenty-six-mile run. He had only to complete a lap of the track and the gold medal would be his. But it was too much for poor Pietre. He was so exhausted and dazed he began running round the track in the wrong direction. He realised his mistake and turned back, but by the time he neared the finishing tape, he'd virtually collapsed. Sympathetic officials rushed forward and helped Pietre the last few metres over the line. He finished first, but because of their help, he was disqualified.

White City Stadium in its dying days – half the stands already gone and the rest soon to follow to the scrapheap.

White City Stadium has seen hundreds of thrilling sporting occasions since then. Many chapters of athletic history have been written on the track and some of the finest British runners have produced their best performances under the glare of the White City floodlights. White City's also played host to sports like show-jumping, stock-car racing, and even World Cup football – one of the matches in the 1966 tournament took place there.

One by one, all those sports found better, more up-to-date venues. In the last few years, it's been greyhound racing that's kept White City Stadium going, but now even the greyhounds have gone for good. Instead of the roars of excited spectators, the only sounds I heard in White City were of the ball and chain and huge pieces of metal and masonry thudding to the ground.

Taking the Stadium apart turned out to be a very big job. The stands that seated the spectators were enormous metal structures built to last and strong enough to be safe. The demolition crew, led by Chris Lewis, had to take each stand to bits using blow torches. I had a go at reducing a steel girder to several smaller pieces. The flame cut through the metal easily enough, but it took time. I realised that demolishing the whole Stadium would take months. Chris's team had a deadline. They'd been hired to do the job by a certain date and they worked long hours to make sure they did.

Once the metal had been cut down to large chunks, bulldozers piled it up into great heaps. I tried my hand at bulldozer-driving and found it very tricky! Getting the bucket on the front and the

Sundin joins the demolition crew! The blowtorch was straightforward, but with me driving the bulldozer, everyone was in danger!

bulldozer acting together took a lot of practice, and Chris didn't have too long to teach me! It was a marvellous feeling being in charge of that great machine, but I thought I'd better leave it to the experts. Demolition sites are no place to fool around in. With so much heavy debris falling down, the strictest safety rules are rigidly enforced.

Those rules certainly applied when Chris and his team brought down one of the huge floodlighting pylons. It stood nearly as high as the Flip Flap all those years ago. The supporting struts were cut away with blow torches and ropes were tied to its legs to ensure it fell into the Stadium and not out across crowded nearby Wood Lane. The bulldozer tugged on the cable and the pylon fell, rushing towards the ground. The noise of the crash echoed and re-echoed across the empty Stadium. Men working on other parts of the ground looked up for a few seconds, then bent down to their blow torches again. They had seen the spectacle before. Soon there would be nothing left of the Stadium at all. It was a sad end for the White City, the Stadium that had seen so much glory, and had such a noble start to life.

GOING, GOING... GONE! The end of a floodlight that's illuminated hundreds of historic sporting moments.

SAFETY FILM 5037
M 5037
SAFETY FILM
SAFETY FILM 5037
►9A
►10
►10A

THE CASE OF THE ASHEN-FACED AUSSIE

Can you solve this case?
Six careless mistakes gave away the crook.
We spotted them. Can you?

The car scrunched across the gravel of the car park and came to a halt under a huge chestnut tree. Former police superintendent McCann, now a globe-trotting private detective, switched off the engine and looked at the beautifully kept field of lush grass that stretched away in front of him.

He turned to his nephew, Bob, who sat beside him in the passenger seat. "So this is Little Bidding," he said. "The home of the Little Bidding Irregulars Cricket Club."

Bob grinned. "That's right. And I hope you enjoy yourself here with us. It's very good of you to come and play for my team here today."

They left the car, collected their cricket bags from the boot, and strolled onto the grass, heading for the distant pavilion. "I'm looking forward to playing," said McCann, placing a white cricketer's sun-hat onto his head. "I had such a hard time with the case of the Hong Kong fat cat and the mystery of his banana plantation, that a peaceful English cricketing day is just what I need."

Bob laughed. "I don't know how peaceful it's going to be," he said. "We're playing against a fiery bunch of Australian players, great lads, a team called Al's Ockers. They'll give us a hard game of it. But we've got one or two surprises of our own – and here comes one of them."

A figure dressed in cricketing whites was coming out to meet them. "Hi Bob!" he called.

"Hi Baz." Bob turned to his uncle: "This is our captain, Barrington Smith. Known as Baz. Born in Barbados, but lived here in Little Bidding for twenty years."

Baz and McCann shook hands warmly: "Glad to have you with us, Mr McCann."

"Great to be here," said McCann. "I look forward to seeing you bowl. If you're from Barbados, you must be a fast bowler."

Baz laughed uproariously. "No way, man. That's what everybody thinks. I never bowl. I bat a bit, I field a bit, that's all."

"Don't you listen to him," said Bob, grinning. "He's a ferocious batsman, and the best fielder in the side. Hit the stumps with a throw from the boundary last week, didn't you, Baz?"

"That was a big fluke," Baz joked, "I was aimin' to hit the batsman, but I missed a little. Hey, man, I must get back to the pavilion. Al's Ockers just arrived, better make them feel at home before we beat 'em. Don't want us to lose on this special day, do we?" He waved an arm and jogged back across the field to the pavilion.

"Special day?" queried McCann.

"Didn't I explain?" asked Bob. "This is the fiftieth anniversary of the founding of the Little Bidding Irregulars. That's why we've got this big match against the Australian lads. It's meant to be a big celebration. Look, here comes our secretary to meet us, in a flap as usual. He's meant to be organising a surprise, as well."

A portly man wearing a panama hat came running up to them, blowing hard. "Here you are, here you are, both of you, splendid, that means we have all 11 chaps here. Well done, you men."

"Hallo, Mr Williams," said Bob. "What about your surprise, then?"

Mr Williams beamed hugely, and lowered his voice. "Guess what?" he said. "I have persuaded the fellows at Lord's to lend us the Ashes, so we can put them on display in the pavilion during the match."

There was an amazed silence. The Ashes are the most treasured object in cricket. When England play Australia at cricket, the victors are said to "win the Ashes". But the actual Ashes themselves are so precious that they never leave the headquarters of world cricket in London.

Mr Williams shuffled nervously. "It's rather a responsibility, what? But the trophy is locked up safe in my suitcase in the pavilion at the moment. I'll unlock it and put the Ashes on display in a few minutes, when the spectators start to arrive, and I assure you, I shan't take my eye off them all day. Even if you score a

century, Bob, I'll keep my position by the Ashes."

"That reminds me, Mr Williams – what number am I batting?"

Mr Williams clapped a hand to his brow. "I'll forget my own name next. The team list is locked up in the suitcase as well. I meant to pin it on the pavilion notice-board. I must do it at once. I'll go and put it on the board right now." He turned and bustled away, his bright, striped tie billowing over his shoulder.

McCann smiled after him. "I must say, Bob," he said, "that a peaceful English Sunday seems much more peaceful when Mr Williams isn't here."

Bob laughed. "He's a fusspot, isn't he, our Mr Williams? But a tireless worker for the club, and a great chap. But you're right about Sundays being so peaceful. We only play on Sundays, it's part of the club tradition. Saturdays are far too hectic for a proper game of cricket."

"Little Bidding Irregulars sound an unusual club," commented McCann.

"Well, we have our ways. Like we never play in league competitions. We just play friendlies. We play seriously, but we don't want to spoil our cricket by getting too serious. A good, well-fought game, and a chat about it all afterwards in the village pub, the Blue Lion."

"Where you talk for hours about who hit the best shot of the day?" asked McCann, smiling.

"That's right. And we'll do the same tonight. It's always Baz that hits the best shots, though. His favourite trick is to hit sixes over the pavilion. You can't see from here, but just behind the pavilion, there's a huge duck pond. If you hit a six over the pavilion, you never see the ball again. Baz reckons to get a dozen balls in there every season."

McCann chuckled heartily as the pair approached the pavilion steps. "I must see if I can't get one or two in the duck pond myself," he said, turning to Bob.

As he spoke, a tall, rangy man crashed into him, and immediately apologised profusely. McCann turned, taking in the man's garishly striped blazer, his cricket cap, the strange manner in which he was holding his right elbow into his side. "I do beg your pardon," he said to McCann. "Fact is, I've just remembered I've left my, er, umbrella in the village pub, you know, the White Horse, and I want to go and get it. Bit worried about it."

McCann turned on the man, with an expression of sudden interest in his face. "I'm sorry to tell you that the pub is closed," he said.

The other man opened his mouth to reply, but before he could do there was a sudden screech of agony from inside the pavilion. Mr Williams came bursting out, his hands clasped to his head in horror: "The Ashes! The Ashes!" he said. "Someone has stolen the Ashes."

There was a long moment of horrified silence. Then McCann turned to the rangy man in the striped blazer and said: "Well, I can't be bothered with that. But I might just be able to persuade the people at the pub to open the door so you can collect your umbrella."

"That's all right, don't put yourself out."

"No trouble. I insist." Something about the way McCann spoke made Bob prick his ears up. "By the way," the detective added, "my name's McCann."

"I'm Hargreaves." The two shook hands. "Good of you to help."

"My pleasure. Do you come here often? I'm a stranger in these parts myself."

Was it his imagination, Bob wondered, or did Hargreaves seem to heave a sigh of relief at this information? Unobtrusively, Bob fell in step alongside the two of them.

"You must come here again," Hargreaves was saying. "I love it here. I'm at Little Bidding almost every Saturday in the season, watching the Little Bidding Irregulars play. Fine bunch of blokes."

"Got some good players, I'm told."

"Absolutely, McCann, old boy. That coloured chap you must have seen running about. He's a brilliant fast bowler, of course. Brilliant."

"They've got some useful batsmen, as well."

"By Jove, they have. Hit the ball all over the shop. Can't count the number of times I've had to slip behind the pavilion to fetch the ball after they've been really playing well."

"They're a good cricket team all right."

"Absolutely, McCann, absolutely. I'm not surprised they're top of the league."

"Well, I hope I don't let them down," McCann said. "I'm playing for them this afternoon, and it's a while since I last had a game."

"McCann, McCann, yes, I thought I'd seen the name before. Yes, you're batting number eight, aren't you? Not a bad berth to choose."

"Could be worse. But they tell me I'll have to be at

my best to score runs against Al's Ockers."

"Do you think you'll beat a side of Australians?" Hargreaves asked. There was something strange, Bob thought, in the way he said this.

"I've no objection to beating Australians?" said McCann. "Have you?"

"You'll never beat any Australians," said Hargreaves. "That's my prediction."

"Think not?" said McCann, with a voice of dangerous quiet. "Then think again. Hand over the Ashes, Hargreaves."

Hargreaves's response was immediate. He took off like a sprinter bursting from the starting blocks, his long legs powered across the green grass of the Little Bidding cricket ground, heading at top speed for the car park, and safety.

"After him, Bob," yelled McCann, setting off in pursuit himself. But Hargreaves was fast – very fast indeed. In ten yards he had doubled his lead. The chase looked hopeless. Already the Ashes looked lost.

"Stop him," McCann shouted. "Stop him!"

Ahead of them, Hargreaves swerved into the car park, and flung himself at the door of his car, desperately scrabbling the key into the lock. It seemed he had won the race for the Ashes by a mile.

And then Baz was running alongside McCann and Bob, not sprinting flat out, but running in a curious, balanced way, stiff-legged, sideways on. "Stop him, Baz!" said Bob. For he had seen what Baz held in his right hand. A cricket ball.

Baz, the crack fielder of the Little Bidding Irregulars, was face to face with the most important moment of his cricketing life. His right arm swung back, and then at once, it flickered like a whiplash, and the red ball was sent skimming like a rocket across the green field of Little Bidding.

It was a long and almost impossible throw, but Baz certainly hit the wicket. The ball crashed exactly in the centre of the windscreen of Hargreaves's car even as Hargreaves was wrenching the door open. The glass shivered into a million cracks, making the window impossible to see through, the car impossible to drive away.

Bob and McCann raced on towards Hargreaves, with Baz close behind. Hargreaves whirled round to face them, defiance blazing in his eyes, but at once he saw he was hopelessly outnumbered.

The car keys dropped from his nerveless fingers. "Pommy blighters! You horrible Poms!" he roared at his pursuers. "You horrible, rotten Poms! Here! Take your rotten Ashes back. I never want to see them again." He lifted his right elbow, which he still held jammed into his side, and the priceless trophy fell from beneath his striped blazer. McCann lunged forward briskly to make a very creditable catch.

"What did you do it for, Hargreaves?" asked Bob.

"I think I can guess," said McCann. "But tell us, Hargreaves."

"I did it for Australia. I did it because I'm an Australian." The phoney English accent had quite gone, and was replaced by rasping Australian vowels. "I wanted to take the horrible Ashes home to Sydney. I'm sick of them being in London. You cheating Pommy blighters – the Ashes belong in Australia by right. You stole them from Australia, and now you've stolen them from me."

McCann turned to see the portly secretary trotting up to them. "Here Mr Williams," McCann said. "Take back the Ashes. And don't take your eyes off them this time."

"My grateful thanks," gasped Mr Williams. "And the eternal thanks of the entire cricketing world. But tell me – how – how did you know Hargreaves was the thief?"

"Bob, you know my methods," smiled McCann. "Tell him."

"He made a mistake", said Bob. "In fact, he made six mistakes, and all of them very foolish."

"And I don't think our truculent Aussie will want to take Englishmen on again in a hurry," observed Mr Williams.

"Or Barbadian men," said Baz, grinning. "C'mon, man, let's go and play cricket. We've got Al's Ockers to beat."

It was left to Bob to sum up. "He hoped to steal the most prized trophy in cricket," he said. "But now it is his own hopes that are in ashes."

Did you spot the six mistakes?
Check your answers on page 76.

THE BOX OF

Who would not wish to own the Box of Delights and experience the mind-blowing feeling of speeding through the air like Kay?

"Whoosh!" he called out in sheer exhilaration when he used the box for the first time to escape from the ravening wolves.

Devin Stanfield is strapped into his Kirby harness by Matthew Kalitowski, watched by the Mouse, played by Simon Barry.

Through the magic of the box, Kay could fly through air, hide in the turn-up of a trouser, and journey back through time. It was easy. But "The Box", as the production team all call it, was one of the greatest challenges BBC Children's Programmes has ever met. How can you produce

something on the television screen which is "magic"? When John Masefield wrote the book, all the magic was in his head, but Renny Rye and Paul Stone, the director and the producer of the series, had to make it all happen before your very eyes!

The actor who played the part

of Kay was a thirteen-year-old schoolboy called Devin Stanfield. He came to the Blue Peter studio to let us into some of the back-stage secrets behind the on-screen magic of *The Box of Delights*.

Dev and Mouse, played by Simon Barry, "flew" into the studio on Kirby wires. This is a trick that

DELIGHTS

two little holes half-covered with fur!" Animal costumes are even older than Kirby wires, but the television special effects are another story. The moment in Episode One when Cole Hawlins with his dog(!) walked into a picture on the wall, climbed onto a donkey's back, and rode away is incredibly complicated that even television directors have difficulty in understanding how it was done.

The magic posed problems for the actors, too. They frequently had to play scenes talking to someone who wasn't there. And although Devin appeared to be small when he had pressed the magic box, in real life he remained his normal height and had to act being a hundreth of the size of Abner Brown.

We put Devin on the spot by asking Patrick Troughton what he thought of his performance of Kay. Patrick, one of Television's most famous actors (remember him as Dr Who?), said simply, "If John Masefield was alive today, he would have chosen Dev to play the part."

No young actor could wish for a greater compliment.

was used long before television was invented. It enabled Peter Pan to fly through the window of the Darlings' nursery when the play was first performed at the Duke of York's Theatre more than 80 years ago! Dev stripped off his jacket and waistcoat to reveal the elaborate harness that the Kirby wire was clipped on to. The magic of television was able to make the wires invisible, and to change the scenery behind Kay so that he would appear to be flying through time and space.

Mouse (Simon Barry) told us his great problems were the intense heat he suffered dressed in his mouse costume under the studio lights, and "just being able to see what was going on through

Devin and the Mouse were joined by Patrick Troughton, the actor who played Cole Hawlins. (Remember him as Dr Who?)

MASEFIELD'S MAGIC BOX

No one can tell how children will grow up. Who could have guessed this three-year-old boy, with his curls and frills, would become a great writer, to chill us all with the mysterious words: "The Wolves Are Running!"

His name was John Masefield – his family called him Jack – and he based the story of Kay Harker, and his battle with the wicked people who try to take the Box of Delights from him, on his own childhood.

1 The Masefields lived in a big house in Ledbury. Jack loved it when their nurse told them stories. *"In those days, as a little child, I was living in Paradise."*

2 *"One wonderful day, when I was five years old, looking at a clump of honeysuckle in flower, life entered into me with a delight I can never forget. I found suddenly I could imagine imaginary beings complete in every detail, and these imaginations did what I wished – for my delight, in a brightness not of this world."*

3 Sadly, life changed. Their mother died, their kind nurse left, and a horrid governess arrived.
"I don't think she was ever kind to us, and we were little beasts to her. I was the worst of them."

5   Things got worse – their father died, too, and an Uncle and Aunt took charge of the six children. The Aunt despised reading; she got rid of all the family books and laughed at Jack's dreams of becoming a writer.

4   They called her The Woman. To escape, Jack hid under the bed in the spare room. *"I was a swift, eager, gluttonous reader, and made up stories of my own, set in deserts, forests, crags, volcanoes, snowy peaks, cataracts."*

7   It was hard going, but Jack worked and got on well. He won a telescope as a prize – but it was for "Writing, Spelling and Composition!"

6   She suggested he should join the Merchant Navy, so 13-year-old Jack became a cadet on the training ship HMS *Conway*.

8   After two years, he was sent to the four-masted sailing barque, *Gilcruix*, bound for Chile from Cardiff. He was dreadfully seasick, and really ill for days at a time.

9   *"The wind beat me against the shrouds, it banged me and beat me, and blew the tears from my eyes with a fury that left me breathless. We got caught in the ice of Cape Horn, and had thirty-two days of such storm and cold as I hope never to see again."*

10   When they reached Chile, Jack was really ill. He spent weeks in a seamen's hospital listening to sailors' stories until he was sent home.

11   Back in England, he passed a wretched winter. The Aunt jeered at him, and insisted he went to New York, by steamship, to join the *Gilcruix* there. *"I felt only hopelessness. The sea seemed to have me in her grip."*

12   When he got to New York, he realised that the Aunt was thousands of miles away, and he was his own master. *"I deserted my ship in New York, and cut myself adrift from her and from my home. I was going to be a writer, come what might."* He had £1 in money and a box of clothes.

13 He tramped the countryside, a homeless vagrant, looking for casual farming work. He went hungry and slept rough, and formed a lifelong sympathy for down-and-outs.

14 He drifted back to New York and took a job in a carpet mill. Years later he wrote a book called *In the Mill*. *"There was a deafening roaring clanging clack, in which one had to shout to make oneself heard, while the appalling ceiling of advancing spools shook and jerked overhead."*

15 He spent his spare time and money in a book shop, and read everything he could. Work at the mill, reading, and his own attempts at writing, filled his life for two years.

16 He wanted to write about ships, the sea and seamen, about down-and-outs, and about the English countryside. At last, sick and almost broke, he got a job on a ship in New York harbour, sailing for Liverpool. *"I was unspeakably, radiantly, burningly happy. My life as a writer was to begin."*

John Masefield was nineteen years old when he got back to England. His wish to become a poet and a great writer came true. When he died, seventy years later, he had been Poet Laureate for thirty-seven years, His memorial stands at Poets' Corner in Westminster Abbey.

He never made another voyage and he was never a tramp again, but he remembered everything he had done, and wrote about it all his life.

In *The Midnight Folk* and *The Box of Delights*, the horrid governess of long ago becomes a wicked witch, and Abner Brown's evil accomplice, Sylvia Daisy Pouncer.

He remembered the delights of the imaginary world he knew as a child but by now John Masefield knew you could never be sure of the Box of Delights – wicked people, or unkind people, would always try to take it away from you.

But in the end, Kay finds himself transported into the magical world of the Box – just as the poet, Jack Masefield, was led to discover again the imaginary world of his childhood.

TOO MANY COOKS...

There's an unusual wooden spoon in the Blue Peter Office, nearly a metre long and polished to a deep mahogany brown. It's far too big to stir a pudding but it sits there as a reminder to Michael and me of the day we stumbled and fell across one of the toughest assault courses in Her Majesty's Armed Forces ... the Royal Marines Cookery Competition!

A field in the middle of Devon on a blustery October day is no place for a picnic. But it's the ideal place for the Competition, which is always held in the open air to make it as realistic as possible. Royal Marine cooks are trained just like other recruits, but they also have to know how to provide hot, nourishing meals quickly to men who might have to spend days surviving in muddy, barren terrain.

Michael and I joined Chef Corporal Gordon Fleet and Marine Driver Chris Bancroft in the Commando Training Centre's "B" team. We were up against nine other teams, including one from the Royal Navy with Leading Wren Colette Hawley – the only other woman competitor. Our task was to cook and present a three-course meal as quickly as possible. The teams lined up alongside their ration packs facing, not their kitchens, but a series of white tapes indicating where their kitchens should be

Kitchen planning, Royal Marine style. Pitching our tent took a lot of cooking time.

Le Menu

Cream of Chicken Soup
avec Croutons

Minced Steak & Kidney Pie
Sausage Savoury
Sauté Potatoes
Petit Pois

Oatmeal Block
avec
Sweet White Sauce

erected. In the Royal Marines, before you cook a meal, you build your kitchen.

"Stand by – GO!" Once the starter's pistol had fired, the whole field burst into life as every team member sprang to the first job. Under Corporal Fleet's direction, we grabbed tent poles and started putting up a frame. Marine cooks also have to be natty tent pitchers! We weren't, and after only ten minutes we were already clearly behind the other teams.

Once we had tables set up inside our tent, the Corporal plonked a five-kilo bag of potatoes in front of me and presented me with a peeler. "Just like home," I thought, "lumbered with the spuds." I attacked the enormous mound with as much energy as I could muster, given that the wind was getting up and blowing straight into our kitchen.

Michael carried on preparing the kitchen for action. With Driver Bancroft he was digging a large trench outside the tent. "For the rubbish?" I enquired. "No," replied Corporal Fleet, "for the flaming oven."

I wondered if my question had made him lose his temper, but when I saw the oven I realised his remark was quite accurate. There's no gas or electricity to connect up to in the middle of nowhere, so the Marines are equipped with a petrol-fuelled field cooker called a Hydro. It's pressurised, and once the nozzle is lit, it looks and sounds more like a flame thrower than a stove. The Hydro went in the hole and a metal cupboard was placed over the top. That's where the food gets cooked, but we would need to watch it carefully to make sure it wasn't burnt to charcoal.

With ten Hydros going full blast around us, Corporal Fleet had to shout his instructions to make himself heard above the racket. "Those peelings are too thick, Janet. We're dicing the potatoes, so slice them lengthways. Quarter of an inch each one." The normal standards of military neatness apply in the Competition, so when Corporal Fleet said "quarter of an inch", I knew that was *exactly* what he wanted. I concentrated on my slicing because in the judging marks would be won or lost on the presentation of food.

Rush, rush, rush! The Hydro is prepared for action, the peel flies off the potatoes, and Michael tries to make the food cook more quickly. Note the hygienic working conditions – luckily no worms dropped in for dinner!

The Hydro was roaring happily away, so Michael tackled the next most important piece of kit – the tin-opener. All the menus have to be cooked with the food available in a ten-man ration pack, and nearly all of that comes out of tins. The Corporal organised the opened tins into courses, and launched into the cream of chicken soup with gusto. I was still knee-deep in spuds, but Super Sundin, the Pastry King, was let loose on the dough for the steak and kidney pie. And the Corporal was able to pass on some of his valuable expertise. "Don't use that knife to break down the margarine. Use your hands, the heat will help soften it. *Not* your palms, that'll melt it, just the tips of your fingers."

Around us other teams were raising red flags to indicate their first courses were ready. Each course is judged separately while it's still hot. Burdened with us, the Corporal's soup was late getting started, so ours was the last red flag to be hoisted. We all left the tent and went out into the rain which had begun to sheet across the Competition site to await the arrival of Warrant Officer Tony Dalton, the Soup Judge. "What sort of things are you looking for?" asked Michael as Mr Dalton prepared to take his first sip. "Colour, consistency, seasoning, taste, and general appearance," was the reply. "On a scale of ten," said Mr Dalton, "I would give your soup … seven!"

More haste, less speed! Michael concentrates on the sausage savouries and Janet carefully sprinkles grated chocolate on the dessert.

I thought that sounded rather good, but our Corporal was a bit crestfallen. I think by that stage he'd resigned himself to the fact that the prized Silver Trophy was not to be his this year.

A vat of potatoes was being sautéed on top of the cooker, and while Michael and Corporal Fleet soldiered on with the main course, I had the chance to show off some of my culinary skills in the preparation of the sweet white sauce for the dessert. Perhaps it

Soup's ready! We wait for judging with a worried-looking Corporal Fleet.

We hear the verdict of Captain Barry Gray, the Main Course Judge, as he samples our steak and kidney pie and sautéed potatoes.

would have turned out a little better if I hadn't stopped halfway through when we raised our white flag for the judging of the steak and kidney pie and the Corporal's secret weapon, his sausage savouries. We were steadily being drenched by this time and it took all our efforts to stop the dinner getting sodden, too. Good presentation is vital, and to my amazement, Corporal Fleet, delving into the bottom of his kitbag, produced silver platters to serve the pie and potatoes on.

The Main Course Judge was Captain Barry Gray. Once again, we were last to be judged. Things didn't start very well. "So this is what we've been waiting for, is it?" said the Captain, peering down at our offering. "It's hot anyway," he

said. But he definitely liked the sausage savouries, and Corporal Fleet looked very proud. And as for my sauté potatoes, all lined up for his inspection, I think he liked those, too.

"If I was walking over these moors and arrived at this, I'd be very pleased," he said. "Yes, I'd be very happy." He chewed a sausage savoury thoughtfully, considering his mark. "Eight" he finally pronounced. "Glad I don't get marked like this at home," I said, "it makes me nervous."

We rushed back to finish the sweet. Not only had all the other teams finished by this time, most had even cleared up and dismantled their tents. I had visions of us trying to coax oatmeal block with sweet white

sauce, sprinkled with grated chocolate, out of the Devon moorside alone, long after dark. Eventually it was finished, and I must say, I thought it looked scrumptious. I was quite confident as Pudding Judge, Captain Bill Walker, came up to us. He sniffed it and took a small mouthful. We smiled at each other.

"It's very nice, but the important thing is they want it with their lunch. It's taken you so long that most Marines wouldn't have bothered waiting." So he didn't give us a mark at all, disqualifying the entry for being so late. All that work! I felt like crying. I can't guess what Corporal Fleet felt like, but he *looked* like he was prepared to throttle us.

All that was left was the presentation to the winners, who turned out to be the HQ and Signals Squadron, Royal Marines. We came last, but we're quite proud of our wooden spoon. Cooking anything more complicated than a bowl of cornflakes under those conditions takes some doing. Perhaps there should have been a special award for Corporal Fleet. He never lost his temper with us, and with a proper team, he would have done a lot better. He showed us that Royal Marine Chefs have a lot of skill, and can turn the most ordinary ingredients into a gourmet's delight!

PEANUT
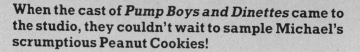

When the cast of *Pump Boys and Dinettes* came to the studio, they couldn't wait to sample Michael's scrumptious Peanut Cookies!

The Pump Boys run the gas station and the Dinettes are the waitresses who work in the snack bar next door, in the first-ever rock musical about a motorway filling station. You can get super meals in America's real Highway Burger Bars, with delicious dishes like Pecan Pie, Cornbeef Hash, Butterscotch Brownies and Cookies – which are what we call sweet biscuits. These Peanut Cookies have a crunchy toasted peanut topping that melts in the mouth – and it's an economical recipe, too. You'll end up with about 20 Cookies if you follow this recipe!

Ingredients

4 oz/100 g butter or margarine
2 oz/ 50 g light, soft brown sugar
6 oz/150 g plain flour
2 oz/ 50 g *unsalted,* roasted peanuts, roughly chopped (or crushed with a rolling pin in a plastic bag)
Pinch of salt
A little milk

Peanut Cookies keep very well in an airtight tin – and taste even better the day after you've made them – but by the time the Pump Boys and the Dinettes left the studio, all *we* were left with was an empty plate!

Recognise the famous faces? See if you can spot who the Pump Boys and the Dinettes are in real life – and turn to page 76 for the answer!

PS **At the time of going to press Peter Duncan had just joined the cast!**

1 Cream the butter and sugar until light and fluffy.
2 Sieve the flour and salt together and stir into the butter and sugar mixture.
3 Mix into a stiff ball of dough and turn on to a floured board or surface.
4 Knead lightly and roll out with a floured rolling pin to approximately 6 mm or ¼ inch thick and cut into circles with a cutter or the rim of a coffee cup or a tin lid (roughly 5 cm/2 inch diameter)
5 Place on a lightly greased baking sheet and brush the tops of the Cookies with a little milk, then sprinkle with the chopped nuts. Press the nuts down, but leave them sticking up above the surface of the Cookies.
6 Bake in a moderate oven (180°C/350°F/Gas Mark 4) for about 12 minutes, or until the Cookies are crisp and golden brown.
7 Leave on the baking sheet for 1 minute then remove and put on a wire rack.

POWDER A PORKER!

MATILDA
TAKE I

"STANDBY!"
You can hear a pin drop on the film set as the director calls for silence. The actors and technicians wait for the sign from the director that brings the huge lights to life. CRAA-AACK, CRAA-AACK, the electricity surges through the bulbs and suddenly the whole set is lit up as if the sun has come out. The actors wait still until the director, absolutely satisfied that everything is just right, calls… "ACTION!!"

The leading lady wanders elegantly on to the set. She fires one of her famous moody glances straight at the camera, and then turns away, pausing only to give a polite OINK-OINK and munch a nearby daffodil…

I was a lucky onlooker at this moment of movie history. I'd heard of pop videos, but I'd certainly never heard of *pig* videos before, not until I went to Firs Farm in Cambridgeshire. Down on the farm, pig breeder extraordinare, John Millard, has brought the video revolution to his sties, transforming his farmyard into Piggy Hollywood.

But like most farmers, John is very level-headed, and there's a good reason for his unusual film set. His herd is so famous – last year it won fifty-five prizes, and had ten champions at the Miss World of Pigdom, the Royal Smithfield Show – that pig farmers from all over the world buy his breeding boars and sows. But if

'BLUE PETER' PIG MOVIES
DIR: ALEX LEGER 1LCH 1475D
42   1
CAM: LAURIE RUSH

Matilda risked getting her nose caught in the clapperboard as she homed in on some food.

you live in Australia, it's a long way to come to Firs Farm to see a pig. So John's idea is to let his customers see exactly what his pigs are like, from the comfort of their own living rooms as they gaze admiringly at his latest pig movie.

Everything has to look its best in a pig video, so I lent John's wife, Jenny, a hand, scrubbing down their newest stars, Winifred and Matilda, getting patches of mud off their sides, and polishing them until they seemed to shine. I was surprised how clean they were in the first place. "They have excellent toilet habits," said Jenny. A clean pig will have separate sleeping and toilet areas in its sty, and a good mother will pass these habits on to her piglets". Winifred and Matilda seemed quite content as we scrubbed them up, rinsed them off, and then applied the final touch – powder. Not

With lights, reflector board and microphone ready for action, John lined up his first shot.

"Look at those muscles in that strong, firm thigh" he said excitedly in the microphone, as Winifred made a dash for the nearest flower beds. "Admire the shape of the snout!" he cried as Matilda buried her nose in a clump of daffodils.

At last when John was satisfied he'd shown all their best points off, they stopped their cavorting for the camera and went back to their sties and a good feed. In a matter of days, John's latest piggy masterpiece was winging its way towards some foreign pig buyer.

John certainly knows a good idea when he sees one, and I, for one, am rather pleased that his pig movies are so successful. It certainly shows all the smart people who live in cities that we farmers don't miss a trick or two either, when it comes to making the most of the latest technology!

John angled himself to capture Winifred's gleaming left flank, as I powdered her backside!

perfumed talcum, but wood dust that showed their lily-white complexion to perfection.

"Standby studio! Winifred and Matilda Scene One! Lights! Camera! ACTION!!" and with Jenny and I waiting to give them a shove if they wandered off the set, Winifred and Matilda began their one and only appearance in films.

John's a one-man band when it comes to the actual videoing. He's his own cameraman and soundman, as well as the director. So while he ordered Jenny and me to get Matilda and Winifred looking the right way, he ran about filming them and added a commentary into the microphone, describing all the pigs' star features.

THE END

The leading lady relaxing with a bite of her favourite food...daffodils.

Safari to Kenya

YOU ARE NOW CROSSING THE

EQUATOR

THIS ROAD WAS BUILT BY H. Z. & CO. LTD.

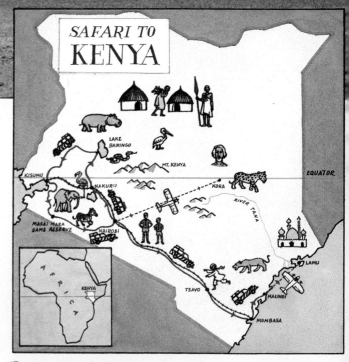

SAFARI TO KENYA

LAKE BARINGO
KISUMU
MT. KENYA
EQUATOR
NAKURU
KORA
RIVER TANA
MASAI MARA GAME RESERVE
NAIROBI
TSAVO
LAMU
MALINDI
MOMBASA

AFRICA
KENYA

In our trusty Safari Truck, we drove hundreds of miles through Kenya's beautiful landscape, crossing the Equator twice.

"Lions!"

"Elephants"

"Wildebeest... and zebras!"

That was the way the conversation went on the flight out to Nairobi, the capital of Kenya. We'd heard all about Kenya's fantastic wildlife and we were really looking forward to our Safari. We knew it would be a once-in-a-lifetime chance to see animals in the wild that normally we would see only behind bars in a zoo.

When we found out from Michael Turner, the Blue Peter film director who'd come out to Kenya ahead of us, that our first trip was to one of the most spectacular wildlife sights in the whole world, we could hardly wait to get aboard our Safari Truck and get going. We were heading for a Game Reserve, but one with a difference. "Not big game," Michael said. "You'll know when you've arrived. Everything turns pink!"

Our destination was Lake Nakuru, 100 miles from Nairobi. It turned out to be one of the most impressive *bird* reserves in Africa. And we soon saw what Michael meant by "pink." The lake is home

for millions of flamingoes. The sight of their shimmering plumage on the water was unforgettable, and a marvellous beginning to our Safari.

The panorama in pink not only looks pretty, it's an example of the perfect wildlife chain in the lake

Beautiful Lake Nakuru, where the elegant flamingoes parade up and down like fashion models. At Lake Baringo, Terry Stevenson pointed out dozens of exotic birds.

itself. Water flows into Nakuru through three inlets, but there are no outlets. That creates a build-up of minerals in the lakebed. Algae – microscopic water creatures – thrive on the minerals, and they in turn provide food for the flamingoes. And the flamingoes aren't pink naturally. There's a pigment in the algae that colours their feathers, so it's almost as if Nature has gone to enormous trouble to provide Lake Nakuru with a beautiful tourist attraction!

There were other species of birds on the lake, too, and we were able to identify pelicans, storks and a very ugly-looking heron without too much difficulty. But, having caught the bird-spotting habit, we needed some expert help to make the most of the dozens of different birds we were seeing, not only on the water, but in trees, reeds, and on bushes at the roadside.

The following day we reached Lake Baringo, 60 miles further north and another bird sanctuary. We tracked down Terry Stevenson, a guide on the lake and a very special ornithologist. Terry's the World Champion Bird Spotter. He won the title by spotting 290 different species in a day, beating the old record by just two. In such experienced company, we looked forward to a vast increase in our knowledge of birds!

Terry took us out on to the lake in his dinghy. He was careful to steer round what

turned out to be a family of basking hippopotami. Like icebergs, most of their bodies were underwater, and they seemed quite harmless despite their huge bulk. But Terry told us about a woman who'd been crushed by a rampaging hippo on the lakeside the previous week, so we were glad he avoided them.

A pink-backed pelican taking off and a roosting red-billed hornbill.

managing to find food for their cattle. The answer was simple, but a sign of the desperation brought on by the drought. The cows were simply herded into the lake itself, to graze on the reeds in the water. That explained why the herders were all carrying spears – there are crocodiles in the lake and a cow would make a tempting target. Although Simon's used to cows, this was a strange experience for him, wading up to his chin in a very smelly lake hoping he wouldn't step on a crocodile!

The Njemps made us welcome. But they're being hit by drought which is destroying the grasslands.

made good use of the binoculars we'd brought along. Terry's eye was so quick, he was able to point out a new bird in every clump of reeds we passed, and we had to keep our eyes skinned to keep up with him. We saw Little Egret, black-winged stilt, Yellow-billed storks, pink-backed pelicans and dozens more. Terry told us that countries like Kenya, around the Equator, are the best in the world for seeing huge varieties of birds. While a keen bird-spotter who never left Britain would do well to see 500 types of birds in a lifetime, there are 1500 to be seen along the whole length of the Equator. We'd certainly got off to an excellent start, and the tips we picked up from Terry gave us a lot of pleasure during the rest of our Safari because we could name many of the exotic birds we saw.

While we were surrounded by Kenya's marvellous birdlife, there was another far more unwelcome companion that we met wherever we drove. It was the drought that Kenya's been suffering for some years, and while we were in Kenya it reached new levels of severity. The signs of drought were everywhere – in the parched fields, the dried-up rivers, and the shrunken lakes. But what it meant to families living off the land was brought home to us the day we went to visit some people of the Njemp tribe.

The Njemps live on the shores of Lake Baringo, in encampments called *menyattas*, but the worsening drought had forced some families to leave the menyattas to go in search of fresh pastures for their herds. We'd made sure we learned a few words of Swahili before we met the Njemps, and once we'd greeted them with *jambo*!, which means hello, we all managed to make ourselves understood.

We arrived in time for the cows' morning feed, and Simon went along to see how the Njemps were

At least it was cool! By mid-morning, the sun was really beating down and Janet soon found herself wishing she was in the lake as well. She joined Nachaki to gather firewood, a task that's a daily chore for the Njemp women.

The Njemps have no coal or oil to make their cooking fires, so they have to search the land for

Janet found wood collecting, back-breaking work.

Elephants and lions, two residents of the Masai Mara.

Driving east, we met George Adamson, the veteran lion expert of *Born Free* fame. He enjoyed the fresh fruit we gave him!

truck into the magnificent Masai-Mara Game Reserve and found that many parts of its seven hundred square miles were brown and bone-dry. But there were still scores of animals to photograph, and as we arrived, we were lucky enough to see one of nature's greatest pageants – the migration of wildebeest from the plains in the south to the fresh grazing in the north. In the drought, the trek was tougher than ever for the wildebeest and only the strongest would survive.

With the help of the Reserve's Senior Warden, we criss-crossed the land, seeking out as many of the fabulous animals as we could. We saw Cape buffalo, giraffe, elephants and zebras. We began to leave the Reserve as dusk fell, and we were both a little disappointed not to have spotted Simon's favourite animal – the lion. But with an incredible stroke of good fortune, we stumbled right on top of a pride of lions. We stopped the truck and watched them, hardly daring to speak. As we sat there, two females broke away from the group to stalk the evening's supper. We tried to keep up with them and luckily found them again. They'd brought down one of the migrating wildebeest and we witnessed the last few seconds of the kill. The lionesses worked as a ruthless team and soon the struggling and squirming of the wildebeest was stilled. It was a chilling experience to watch, and yet it was one more reminder of the balance and wisdom of nature. That scene would be repeated scores of times that very evening all over the Masai-Mara, and yet there would still be millions of wildebeest that would survive. their long trek to the north.

When we returned to Nairobi, there was one place we couldn't wait to see. The boys' school at Starehe is one of the miracles of modern Kenya. It began life twenty-five years ago as a couple of tin huts, providing shelter to some of the waifs that roamed the city streets at night. Today, it's the most famous and respected school in Kenya. Poor boys are still given shelter and an education, but rich families also queue up to send their children to Starehe. To outsiders, it's impossible to tell who's been rescued from poverty, and who has a wealthy family. So, once a

wood. But as the land is stripped of trees, the topsoil is eroded, gradually turning it into desert and stopping crops from ever growing there again. It's a sad story that's being repeated across Africa. It's adding to the spread of the deserts and making the drought worse because the land can't retain what little rain there is.

It's remarkable how cheerful all the Njemps were, considering the awful plight they're in. The lake is the key to their lives, and if it were to continue receding it wouldn't be able to keep the families going any longer. We were able to leave at the end of the day in our Safari truck, but for the Njemps there is no easy way of escaping the crisis. As we drove away, we had no idea that less than four months later, Simon would be back in Africa, seven hundred miles to the north in Ethiopia reporting on the devastating famine there.

The wild animals also suffered in the drought. We took our safari

whole school, has a special connection with Blue Peter, and that was an extra reason for our visit. In 1971, Valerie Singleton accompanied Princess Anne, when the Princess visited Starehe in her capacity as President of the Save the Children Fund. The 1971 Blue Peter Appeal provided two dormitories for 60 boys at the school, and ever since then we've tried to keep up our close links with Starehe. Joseph was interviewed by the Princess and Valerie in the Place of Safety, the rescue centre where destitute boys stay until they're either accepted into the school, returned to their homes, or resettled. He's come a long way since then, and has good reason to love the school that changed his life.

Joseph showed us the Blue Peter Dormitories, not dormitories any more, but now badly-needed

Princess Anne and Valerie Singleton visiting Starehe in 1971.

boy leaves, there's no stigma or disgrace attached to a Starehe education. In fact, it's an honour.

We visited Starehe the day after the twenty-fifth birthday

The games room was built thanks to Blue Peter viewers, and the programme was honoured in Starehe's birthday parade.

recreation rooms. Larger residence blocks have been built since 1971 to show how the school, and the people behind it, are always willing to progress and move on. In the games room, we met today's generation of Starehe pupils, playing table-tennis, reading, and concentrating on a draughts-like game called Ajua. We also helped dish up lunch, and it was quite a shock for two people who used to moan about their school dinners! We gave every boy a fresh baked roll and a fizzy drink, and that was it! But they get a good, hot meal every evening. Later, Simon joined a soccer game, hoping that a lifetime supporting Derby County would somehow rub off and let him teach the boys a thing or two. But playing in the thin air at 5000 feet above sea level left him gasping out on the wing!

We were delighted to have renewed the links with Starehe, and hope they will always remain close. Kenya itself will forever have a special place in our hearts. The welcome given by the people, the stunning scenery and the enormous variety of wildlife make it a country to remember. Let's hope it won't be too long before we're saying *Jambo*! again.

celebrations, and everyone was fairly glowing with pride at the praise heaped upon the school by, among others, the President of Kenya, Mr Daniel Arap Moi. The President had even hinted at an exciting new development – a Starehe for *girls*. That would be a breakthrough because girls get even less education than boys in Kenya.

We met Joseph Kingala, a Starehe boy who's gone on to become a teacher at the school. He, and the

THE HOUSE WHERE TIME STOOD STILL

"Go upstairs and tidy your room!" How many times have you heard that? But no one ever said it to the Harpur-Crewes.

When I have a big tidy-up, it always seems terribly boring at first, but when I actually get started, I find lots of things I'd forgotten all about, and it becomes really fascinating.

But imagine a house where no one has thrown anything away for more than a hundred years!

I found just that when I went to Calke Abbey.

It was difficult to find through the winding lanes. Unlike many stately homes, there were no conspicuous signposts, no huge car parks or streams of visitors. Calke Abbey lay almost hidden in a quiet parkland where grazing deer were the telling me the story of the house and the family, and why it is like nowhere else in the world.

As we walked along corridors and up stairs, we passed case after case of seagulls, songbirds and owls, until we reached the Salon, a fine, impressive room – but with more birds in every corner.

The third Sir Henry Harpur-Crewe was a shy man who hated people – his neighbours called him "the isolated baronet". But he was an enthusiastic naturalist, and he paid to have countless birds stuffed and put in glass cases. Many of his descendants were keen on stuffing birds, too. It was all naturalists could do before filming was invented – but it does mean that Calke Abbey is a kind of bird nightmare.

In 1856 the Lady Harpur-Crewe of the time "did up"

Mr Harpur-Crewe led me upstairs in the house that his family has lived in for more than three hundred years. It was like nowhere else in the world.

the drawing room in the height of Victorian splendour, all ready for visitors, but sadly, the Harpur-Crewes had such a reputation for being recluses, and disliking company, that visitors never came.

"I might be allowed to be more like other people and have a few friends sometimes, it would cheer me and do me good," lamented the poor lady.

So the drawing room was left, smart and untouched, with heavy carved furniture and hundreds of elaborate ornaments. It is a time capsule of Victorian life, and historians want it to stay that way for ever, as fresh as the day it was completed.

Not all the rooms look so fresh and cared for. As we lifted iron bars and drew back shutters more than 350 years old, the light pierced the gloom and I could just see a jumble of junk and furniture, toys and treasure, and dusty school books that had lain undisturbed for years and years.

There was a schoolroom where children who did not go to an ordinary school, spent day after day learning lessons with their governess.

There were bright pictures illustrating Bible stories, and a doll's house which was probably made on the spot by the estate carpenter. I could imagine how wonderful it had been when the paint was

only sign of life. The walls of the house have stood for centuries, and a sundial outside the front entrance has marked the passing years of family history.

When I stepped into Calke Abbey, I felt rather scared. There seemed to be no one about, and the entrance hall was lined with the heads of deer and long-horned cattle, who didn't seem particularly pleased to see visitors.

There was a warm fire, though, and when Mr Harpur-Crewe, the present owner of Calke Abbey, appeared, he gave me a very warm welcome. He took me all round his family home, gleaming, and before the furniture got broken.

Probably the very favourite was the Noah's Ark – children were allowed to play with it on Sundays when their other toys were locked away, because it was based on a Bible story. I began to arrange the pairs of crudely painted animals in a procession, and I wondered how many years it was since children played in that shadowy room, cut off from the world outside.

Mr Harpur-Crewe's family first came to Calke Abbey in 1622. The last baronet was his grandfather, Sir Vauncey Harpur-Crewe, who was named after a remote medieval ancestor. There are photographs of him all round the house. They show a serious little boy, who grew up to be a recluse and a naturalist, like so many of his family.

The bedroom he had as a little boy still exists, chilly and forbidding now, but still full of his treasures – a toy horse and cart, sporting guns, and case after case of moths and butterflies, all

The doll's house that was played with by children cut off from the world outside.

The generations of naturalists had turned the house into a bird nightmare.

beautifully arranged.

When the Harpur-Crewes wanted a change, they didn't redecorate – they just took over an empty room. It must have been like the Mad Hatter's Tea Party, with everyone moving on, which is why the rooms are so fascinating, like the one with a four-poster bed and a cupboard full of beautiful little girls' dresses, covered with lace and embroidery.

When Sir Vauncey was owner of Calke Abbey, he refused to make any changes in the house he loved, and although by now it was the twentieth century, he would never allow a motor car or any other motor vehicle to enter the park.

His son, Richard, was very different. Cars and steamboats and aeroplanes were his passion, and he even decorated his room with them. He would surely have brought Calke Abbey into modern times, but sadly, it was not to be.

He died before his father, and when Sir Vauncey died in 1924, a very old man, Richard's sister, Hilda, who is the present Mr Harpur-Crewe's aunt, inherited the Abbey and the title of baronet died out.

When Mr Harpur-Crewe took over, the Inland Revenue were demanding £8,000,000 in tax and he could only get that money by selling Calke Abbey, which meant it would go out of his family for ever.

But now the National Trust is going to take over the house as a National treasure. Mr Harpur-Crewe will be allowed to carry on living there, and the public will be able to see this extraordinary house for themselves.

It will take several years, to mend the roof, clean it all up and put in proper lighting and heating. I am very glad it will be preserved, and I hope to go there again – but I shall never forget when I was the only visitor, and the wintry sunshine lit up toys which had not been played with for a hundred years.

Below this strange house lie the kitchens – and on the wall is a message to the cook and her staff: "Waste not, want not." I wonder if this is why the family living upstairs never threw anything away. Alongside the message is a huge clock, long stopped, which could be the symbol of all those isolated baronets who have lived at Calke Abbey – the House Where Time Stood Still.

The clock which could be the symbol of the house where time stood still.

The Age of Steam has a ring to it. The great panting effort, the sudden hiss, the plume of black smoke – in fact, the very smell of a steam locomotive can set the pulses racing, and make the high-speed train look puny by comparison. No one feels this more than Brell Ewart who hails from Ashbourne in my native Derbyshire. Brell, to put it politely, is a railway enthusiast – some would call him a railway buff – others a railway nutter. The fact is, he eats, drinks, thinks and sleeps steam locomotives.

When the diesel engines really took over, hundreds of magnificent old steam locos were dumped on scrap-heaps like rusting graveyards throughout the country.

080

"The old boiler-smiths spent every day of their lives crouched up like that," Brell told me. Can you imagine it? You wouldn't get anyone to do the job nowadays!

Except for Brell and his mates, that is.

There was fur all over the side of the boiler, like a huge, old kettle. Brell handed me another gun that

Brell and his band of fellow enthusiasts watched and waited until they heard of an engine that had the class, and contained sufficient challenge to make it worth dedicating five years of their lives to restoring. They found 80080 on a dump in South Wales in 1981 and brought her up the M1 on a low-loader to Matlock where the labour of love began. I have paid two visits to the 80080 – one in 1982 when work first started, and one last winter. And the head of steam created by the roaring enthusiasm of Brell and his mates had not been damped down by their three years' hard slog. As soon as I arrived, Brell had me hammering rivets into place with a compressed air gun. The rivets are heated up by a gas burner until they're red-hot, and then passed like fury to the rivetter who only has seconds to hammer them home before they cool down.

We squeezed through a narrow hole into the cavernous, rusting inside of the boiler. I felt very shut in as I crouched with Brell on the concave floor. It was like being inside a huge drainpipe.

I disappeared into the bowels of the cavernous old boiler.

activated a dozen steel needles which spiked off the furry deposit. The noise inside the iron tube was beyond the threshold of pain.

The boiler had been separated from the loco chassis whilst it was being restored, and today they were going to be reunited to make 80080 look like a proper

Inside the boiler was furred up like an old kettle. Brell showed me how to descale it.

Using another restored locomotive, I shunted the steam crane into position.

locomotive again. As the boiler weighs about 15 tonnes, we needed some help, and what could be more appropriate than a massive, restored steam-crane which would have done the job 50 years ago.

I shunted the beautiful old machine along the track using one of the already restored steam locomotives. Positioning the crane by the 80080 was crucial.

The wheels of the crane were locked off and the outriggers to stabilise the 130-tonne beast were cranked into position.

"There are only three of these left in the country, Simon," Brell told me as we stoked up the fire. Eric Riley, the crane driver, presided over a row of enormous, gleaming steel levers that controlled the crane jib. Everything built at the beginning of the century had to be big, and so they needed big men to operate the machinery. Today's cranes are controlled by fingers on a joy-stick. They are, of course, better than the old machines, but I wonder if the men who work them get the same feeling of

Slowly, inch by inch, the boiler lurched towards the chassis.

satisfaction which Eric obviously enjoyed as he slammed the huge levers home.

The great jib slowly began to rise, lifting the 15-tonne boiler almost with an air of nonchalance. It hung swinging over the chassis which had now to be shunted into position with hairbreadth accuracy. The holes had to line up with the bolts with absolute precision. There were lots of "Whoas – back a bit – Come on, Charlie", before Brell lifted up his hand and called:

"Right, that's it! Bring her down slowly, Eric."

Eric eased over one of his

levers, the great crane hissed with power, and very slowly, we manhandled the huge boiler home on its chassis once again.

Brell and I jumped off the engine and stood back to survey our handiwork.

"Looks a bit more like a loco now, Simon," he said, in his flat, matter-of-fact Derbyshire voice. But there was no mistaking the gleam of delight shining through the eyes beneath the greasy cap.

"You must come back next year when we should have her steamed up," he said.

"Brell, I wouldn't miss that for the world," I said. And I meant it.

The outriggers to stabilise the crane were cranked into position.

RADIO ROBOTS

If Bill and Ben had been radio-controlled – who knows – they might have escaped from their kidnappers!

The very first radio-controlled models were tried out in America and Britain in the mid 1930s, and the cream of the inventions are always displayed at the Model Engineer Exhibition that's held at Wembley directly after Christmas. For people lucky enough to live near London, it's a good treat for the Christmas holidays, and this year there was a bonus for Blue Peter viewers – anyone who visited the Exhibition wearing their Blue Peter badge was allowed in free of charge!

Sometimes the exhibits are mind-bogglingly complicated. Dedicated modellers spend years perfecting the smallest details of clocks, locos, ships, miniature

I'd never seen a *moving* dinosaur's skeleton before!

cars, and even working Spitfire engines! The Gold and Silver medals awarded to the best models are highly prized, all over the world.

The electronics can be fairly complicated, but the charm of Paul Jefferies models is they're so realistic, you forget about the engineering and just enjoy the novelty of the way his huge, furry caterpillar crawls with its back gently arching up and down – just like the real thing. By sending radio signals to its built-in

I enjoyed working Paul Jefferies' unusual models – especially arching the Caterpillar's back.

receiver, you can also make its head move and furrow its bushy eyebrows over its large, ping-pong ball eyes. He looked really funny and Goldie couldn't make him out at all!

Paul Jefferies brought three more of his radio-controlled models to the studio – a little old man on a bicycle, a funny lady waving her stick in a fury, and a dinosaur with radio-controlled feet, neck and head! They were a great change from the highly technical exhibits that model-makers usually produce, and we can't wait to see what Paul Jefferies comes up with next year!

COOL CATS

Jack was in the company of 200 other felines one memorable day last November – and they gave him a lesson in good behaviour – they didn't budge an inch!

I haven't always liked cats. Before I joined the cast of the *Cats* musical, I thought they were dull and boring. But to act and dance the part of Bill Bailey, I had to put a bit of homework in. I spent a lot of time watching cats and kittens, reading all about them and looking at paintings, photos and sculptures. It didn't take me long to discover how wrong I'd been! Cats are intelligent and beautiful, and I became the proud owner of two white Persian kittens, Caesar and Cleo! On Blue Peter, although he still does his famous disappearing act, Jack will sit on my lap for quite long spells – I think cats can always sense when people like them.

The cast bronze models varied in height from 2.5 to 7.5 centimetres. Altogether the whole collection fetched £20,593 when it was auctioned at Phillips.

This cat photographer was sold for £240.

The owner of this collection of models must have been cat crazy! They came from Austria where they were made between 1880 and 1920, and you name it – there's a cat doing it! There were sleeping cats and eating cats – cats having a cuddle and playing pianos – even a whole cat orchestra. There were dancing cats and cats riding bikes – cats perched on roof-tops and playing ring a ring o' roses. Some of them were very athletic – like the cat rowers having a race, and the ones that especially caught my eye were the acrobatic cats, as there was even a kitten jumping through a hoop.

The models are cast bronze sculptures and the biggest is only 7.5 centimetres tall. Although they're so tiny, they're amazingly realistic and the technique that gives them their almost lifelike appearance is called cold painting, which means they're painted *after* the bronze has been cast.

The cats' owner must have spent years collecting them, and it's sad to think that now they're divided up and belong to dozens of different people. A few days after we showed the collection on the programme, it was auctioned at Phillips. I'd have given my left arm to have owned just one of the models – but no such luck! Phillips estimated they'd fetch between £30 and £300 *per cat*, and the 150 lots eventually raised a staggering £20,593! The top price paid was £700 for the orchestra, complete with an upright piano.

Perhaps one day someone will make a model of Jack for our shelves – like our lovely sculpture of Petra. But he'll have to learn to sit still – otherwise the sculptor will have a cat-astrophe on his hands!

I liked the acrobatic cats best of all. They reminded me of my tumbling in the Boy George video!

Lee Boo

Just imagine what it would feel like to come to London from a tiny island, thousands of miles away – and with no TV or films or books to tell you what England was like. 200 years ago, that's what happened to the young Prince of a Pacific island. He came as a visitor to Rotherhithe, on the River Thames – a couple of miles downstream from Tower Bridge. His name was Lee Boo, and when I visited Rotherhithe, I discovered the people who live there still remember his extraordinary story that began on the other side of the world.

1   In August of 1783, as the ship *Antelope* with its Captain, Henry Wilson, was sailing back to England laden with rich goods from China, it was wrecked on a coral reef. Captain Wilson ordered his crew ashore. They were off the Pelew Islands in the Pacific Ocean and they were terrified because they'd heard the inhabitants were fierce fighters, even cannibals!

2   When they reached the island Oroolong, they found the islanders lined up with their Rupack, or King, at their head. They were a fearsome sight, with fuzzy hair and painted bodies. Yet they welcomed the sailors in the kindest way, and gave them food. Luckily, one of the crew spoke Malay, and one of the islanders was a Malayan, shipwrecked two years before, so they acted as interpreters.

3   Prince Lee Boo, the Rupack's 19-year-old son, was very interested in the Englishmen. He learned some English and he and the other islanders helped the sailors build a new boat.

4   The Rupack asked Captain Wilson if he would take Lee Boo back to England to learn things he could teach the islanders, and Captain Wilson promised to treat him like his own son.

5   The Islanders loaded the boat with food and presents, Captain Wilson nailed a copper plaque to a tree to record their visit, and Lee Boo (feeling strange in English clothes) said "Goodbye" to his father.

6   They arrived in Portsmouth on 14 July 1784. The journey had lasted for eight months and by now Lee Boo was ten thousand miles from home. He and Captain Wilson travelled to London by coach. "We have been put into a little house and run away with by horses!" Lee Boo exclaimed.

7   When they reached Captain Wilson's house at Rotherhithe, his wife and his son, Harry, were as kind and welcoming as the Pelew Islanders had been to the English sailors. Soon Lee Boo was great friends with Harry and devoted to the lady he called "Mother Wilson".

8   Soon Lee Boo was a familiar sight in Rotherhithe. When he passed a frail old man, he pressed money into his hand. "Must give poor old man, old man no able to work," he explained to Harry.

9   He went to Rotherhithe Academy and worked hard learning to read and write English. "My father think me very wise when I go home and teach great people their letters," he said.

10   He wasn't perfect all the time. Once he started to teach Harry spear-throwing in the attic, which must have alarmed Mrs Wilson very much.

11   When he was free, Captain Wilson took them to see the guards at St James's Palace. Lee Boo loved that.

12   This happy, busy life went on for five months. Then, very sadly, Lee Boo caught smallpox. "Lee Boo do well, Mother," he said bravely to Mrs Wilson, but he knew he was very ill and he asked them to tell his father how happy he had been in England.

RUPACK ST.

13   Prince Lee Boo died on 27 December 1784. All Rotherhithe attended his funeral, and it was said: "Every person in the family wore the face of grief."

Lee Boo had only lived in Rotherhithe for five months, but everybody loved him, and he is still remembered there – not far from St Mary's Church, Rupack Street was named in his memory.

Most of old Rotherhithe has gone now, but Lee Boo would still recognise St Mary's – he came here every Sunday with the Wilsons. There's a memorial plaque to him inside, and in part of the churchyard that's now a children's playground,

you can see where he is buried – next to the family he loved so much. The words on his tomb read: "To the memory of Prince Lee Boo, son to Abbe Thulle, who departed this life on the 27th December, 1784" – and there's a little poem written there:
"Stop, reader, stop, let nature claim a tear.
A Prince of mine, Lee Boo, lied buried here."

When Simon invited me to his parents' farm in Dethick, I quickly accepted, looking forward to a nice, lazy weekend in the country. And I wasn't disappointed by the way things started, sitting in the cosy kitchen munching home-made fruit cake made by Mrs Groom. It was when Simon took me outside to look at the fields that I began to suspect he might be hiding something up his sleeve. In no time at all, any ideas I had about a restful holiday vanished into the Derbyshire air ...

"Ever dipped a sheep, Michael?"

We were gazing at a field containing a great many sheep when Simon popped that question. I didn't have a clue what he was talking about. There *aren't* many sheep in Gateshead! I asked Simon to explain.

"A lot of sheep have been catching a dreadful disease called scab over the last couple of years. Now all the sheep farmers have to round up their flock twice a year for a special bath in disinfectant – and today's bath day!"

Simon's Dad joined us and pointed out the different varieties of sheep: Jacobs, Suffolks and Mashams. There were also some brown sheep, a cross between the Jacobs and Suffolks. In all, I counted about three hundred sheep and I began to look forward to the work. It wasn't what I expected,

It took a lot of skill and patience to round up three hundred frisky sheep.

but it was going to be fun. But before you can dip your sheep, you've got to catch them.

We were strung out in a line across the field: Mr Groom, me, Simon and Simon Grant, a local lad who was helping out. Goldie was no help at all. She was romping across a distant hillside with her daughter, Lady, who lives on the farm. Instead, we had a real sheepdog, Bob, to help us. It took some time as the sheep seemed very skilled in running just where you *didn't* want them. I yelled the same

The sheep had to be coaxed one by one towards the bath.

rest of the flock through. But the decoy had no power to attract the first stubborn sheep, so Simon Grant bustled up to lend me a hand. Between us we got the animal moving towards the drop into the bath. It took a few steps more, then *splash!* Simon deftly hooked the sheep by the neck with his Dad's shepherd's crook, and gently pushed its head underwater. The sheep struggled for a few seconds, then half-swam and half-stumbled up and out of the pool, shaking itself dry. One dipped sheep, two hundred and ninety-nine to go!

It was very hard work at the shoving end of the line, and after a while Simon asked me if I'd like to take a turn with the shepherd's crook, dipping the sheep. "Be careful to push them right under, Michael," Simon said. "It may look painful for them,

The curved end of the shepherd's crook made sure the sheep weren't hurt while they were dipped in the bath.

commands as the others, and after a lot of "go on there" and "get away, get away", we managed to get the whole flock into the yard.

I helped Simon add the strong-smelling disinfectant to the water in the bath. There was a line of pens to channel the sheep through to the pool. It seemed simple enough, but as soon as we started on the real work, I found things very difficult. No matter how hard I shoved, I couldn't get the first sheep even to budge. Simon had already lifted a sheep, called a decoy, to the other side of the bath, to help tempt the

PC Gibbs arrived to ensure we obeyed all the sheep dipping regulations.

but it's a lot better than catching sheep scab."

So under they all went – even the little lambs. Simon told me that the disinfectant kills the miscroscopic ticks and lice that get under the sheep's skin. Once a sheep gets scab, it loses most of its wool and it can even die. A dunking in a cold bath seemed a small price to pay to avoid that.

We'd been dipping some time, and the number of sheep having their wool dried in the autumn sun was steadily growing when Simon spotted a visitor to the farm. "Look, there's a Bobby coming!"

I was a bit surprised to see a policeman and wondered if something was wrong. But Constable Gibbs had come along to enforce the very strict rules about sheep dipping. He had to make sure the liquid in the bath was the correct strength, for instance. "You don't test it personally?" joked Simon.

The constable stationed himself in a strategic position where he could watch all the proceedings. I noticed he was keeping a careful eye on me – it didn't take him long to work out I'm not a farming boy. Soon he was calling out to me. "Just try and keep them in a little bit longer, will you? A full minute with their heads fully under at least once!"

After three and a half hours, I found myself pushing the very last sheep through the pen and into the bath. Once dipped, it joined the others, and we released the whole flock into a small field – the little

Smile! A flock of gleaming sheep pose for a snap!

lambs leading the way. The sheep seemed to be glowing. And they were, compared to us! We were absolutely filthy and smelly, and covered in sheep dip which was dripping off our clothes.

Mr Groom signed the form that Constable Gibbs brought with him, stating that he'd obeyed all the regulations, and all of us had a thoroughly well-earned mug of tea with three hundred sheep grazing happily nearby. It had been a messy and very wet introduction to life on a farm, but at least it had shattered any illusions I'd had about the quiet life they lead in the countryside!

The best cup of tea I've ever tasted – it looked more inviting than the sheep dip. Even the copper got a cuppa!

CABLE CAR CAPERS

You might think that a freefall parachute jump from 12,500 feet would cure anyone from a fear of heights. Think again!

Dangling one hundred and seventy metres above the Derbyshire countryside with nothing between you and the ground is a very bad time to discover you're terrified of heights. But that's exactly how I felt when I reported from Britain's first Alpine-style cable car system.

It's suspended above the Heights of Abraham, a beautiful, wooded hillside that rises sheer over the village of Matlock Bath in Derbyshire. Climbing the Heights has always been a problem. The Victorians tried using donkeys, but on the whole, visitors have had to rely on a stout pair of walking shoes. The cable car idea was born as the Heights were being smartened up. The system took seven months to build and now visitors have the opportunity to ride to the top and see the spectacular views.

I met Barry Thompson, the cable car manager, in the base station, where he showed me the heart of the system – the enormous bull-wheel which is powered by an electric motor. Barry has complete faith in the mechanism. But I couldn't help having a few doubts.

The bull-wheel hauls the thick cable up and down the line.

Barry checked my harness thoroughly.
He didn't want us to part company!

I pumped awa
on the grease
container so
Barry could
service the
rollers.

"What happens if there's a power cut?" I asked him.

"We hope it will never happen – but, just in case, we've got a standby diesel engine."

Barry told me it takes careful and regular maintenance to keep everything running smoothly. I joined him on a routine service run, going up the cable in the little open maintenance basket.

In no time we were high above the hillside with Matlock Bath spread out below us. We were heading for Tower Two, one of the enormous pylons that carries the cable. As the tower loomed up before us, the ground seemed a very long way down – and it was – one hundred and seventy metres!

An instruction from Barry over the walkie-talkie brought the maintenance basket gently to a stop right under the top of the tower. The only movement was the platform swinging in the wind which was rather strong, but Barry had no hesitation in leaving the basket and climbing up the tower to get to the cable rollers. As soon as Barry was sure the rollers were well lubricated, he came back to the basket and we moved off down towards the base station again.

Don't panic! Rescue is on the way as Ellis slips down the cable.

The cable cars were a welcome sight after the scary ride on the ski lift chair.

If the worst *does* happen, and a passenger car is suddenly stranded halfway up the Heights, there's a special emergency device launched from the Top Station at the summit of the cable car ride. It's a bit like a ski-lift chair and the occupant holds on while the chair whirrs down the cable to whoever needs rescuing. The minute I sat in it, I knew it was ten times worse than the maintenance platform.

But Barry hadn't deserted me. He was on his own chair about ten metres behind, and as we neared the car playing the part of the stranded victim, he yelled instructions to me. I drew up alongside the cable car and clambered on to the roof. A door opens into the car, and I managed to swing my legs through it.

"Right! Get your hands round the hatch and slide down into the seat!" Barry commanded. He arrived behind me, and as I slid into the cable car, he undid the safety strap that was holding me to the ski-lift chair. With a thump I landed in the cable car, very relieved to have got there in one piece.

If this had been a real emergency, it would be my job to winch the stranded passengers to the ground. But on this occasion, I was the first one down to the ground, tied to a rope. I couldn't honestly say that the prospect of landing was more difficult than when you're parachuting, but as my last parachute landing had put me in hospital, I was very careful about touch-down on the Matlock hillside. Luckily, this time there were no bones broken – just relief at having got down safely.

Two hundred thousand people rode in the cable car during the summer of 1984. None of them tried out that ski lift though … and that's one assignment for Blue Peter that I'm *not* intending to repeat. Give me parachuting any day – broken pelvis and all!

LUNA PEDES

Our Galactic Lunapedes may not be as big as Paul Jefferies' radio-controlled caterpillar, but they're lovely movers, and they're a lot less complicated! The more you practise manipulating their strings, the more you can make them do and you don't have to build Space scenery for them – they're lots of fun on their own. And in the true Blue Peter tradition – they don't cost an arm and a leg to make – all you'll need is an old ping-pong ball, some buttons and beads, a cotton reel and some old lolly sticks.

1   For the Lunapede's head, make two eyeholes in a table-tennis ball just above the join line – about 2-3cm apart.

Use a bradawl to make the holes, but take great care – you may need an adult to help with this bit. Enlarge the holes with a small pair of nail-scissors.

2   Make a hole for the neck on the opposite side of the ball from the eyes, and a fourth hole in the top of the ball for the antennae.

3   A good tip for painting the head is to push a straw or stick into one of the holes to keep the ping-pong ball steady while you paint it. We used silver paint – but any colour will do. Stand the straw in a jar while the paint dries.

4 Paint the various parts of the Lunapede's body before you fix them together (they don't have to be exact copies of these!)

5 Thread a 30-cm length of wool through a needle and down through one hole of a large button to the underside, then up through the other hole, leaving enough wool at the end to tie a couple of knots to secure the button in place.

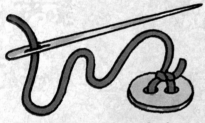

Thread the wool through a large bead and then fix the second large button to the end of the strand in the same way as before. Trim off the spare ends of wool. Make a second pair of legs to match.

6 Use a 50-cm length of thin elastic or string to hold the body sections together.

Push an end of the elastic through the large bead on one of the pairs of legs.

Take both ends of the elastic together and push them through the cotton reel.

7 Push one end of the elastic through the large bead on the second pair of legs, and push the other end of elastic through the bead in the opposite direction. Pull the ends of elastic tight so that all the body sections are held close together.

8 Thread both ends of the elastic through a medium-sized bead and then through a bodkin.

Push the bodkin into the neck hole of the head and out through the hole at the top.

9 Finally, thread the two ends of elastic through the last bead and pull them up tight. Tie the ends together firmly and make several knots so that the elastic will not slip through.

Trim the ends of elastic to the same length and separate them for antennae.

10 For the eyes, push the shanks of small buttons into each eyehole. (If you don't have buttons with shanks, glue them in place.)

11 The frame that holds the puppet strings is made from three ice lolly sticks, glued to form an H.

12 The six puppet strings are lengths of sewing thread.

The thread that holds the head is sewn through the elastic knot (a), at the base of the antennae.

The thread that holds the back end of the body is tied between the bead and cotton reel (b).

Fix the ends of these strings to the ends of the central lolly stick using small strips of sticky tape.

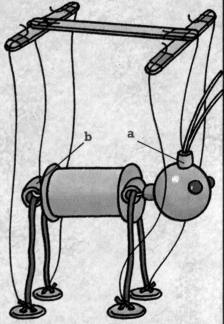

For the feet strings, sew threads through the knots that hold the buttons in place. Fix the other end of these threads to the ends of the other lolly sticks, using sticky tape.

Leave the ends of the threads loose so that they can be pulled under the tape to adjust the length.

PS If the strings get badly tangled you can simply peel off the sticky tape, untangle the threads and re-fix them!

Now find a mirror!

Puzzle Pictures

1 Each year the **Lewes Borough Bonfire Society** builds a giant Guy Fawkes – **the 1984 Guy towered 4.97 metres!**

2 **Mud Race!** Relaxing on the banks of the River Exe after a mile-long race across the mud flats.

3 An anxious moment as magician **Paul Kieve** chopped Janet in three!

4 We all dressed in 1940's clothes and turned into **the Modernaires – Tex Beneke's** backing group – for **Glenn Miller's Chattanooga Choo-Choo!**

5 A strangely silent **Boy George** created by Kevin Plumb for the **World of Wax Museum in Great Yarmouth.**

6 **The world's oldest diving suit** – made in Finland over 200 years ago.

7 Which dog is alive? Answer: Goldie! **The Old English Sheepdogs were knitted by Mrs June Davis!**

8 Goldie's 3-D portrait created from **string by artist Bill Orton.**

9 The one-seater plane built for **Oxfordshire's Village Enterprise** week. A draw was held to guess how far it would fly!

10 **"Living Sculpture"** – an unusual form of mime invented by artist **Duncan Whiteman.**

11 **Dipak Pancholi** of Leicester, playing the part of **Hanuman the Monkey God** in the Abbey Primary School's celebrations for **Diwali – the Hindu Festival of Light.**

Peanut Cookies

The first cast of **Pump Boys and Dinettes** was Paul Jones, Kiki Dee, Carlene Carter, Brian Protheroe, Gary Holton and Julian Littman.

The case of the Ashen-faced Aussie

1 McCann's suspicions were first aroused when Hargreaves said he had left his umbrella in the White Horse. The village pub is called, as Bob said, the Blue Lion. Hargreaves had said he was a regular at the Little Bidding games. Plainly he was lying.

2 Once McCann had said he was a stranger to Little Bidding, Hargreaves tried to explain his presence there by pretending to be a regular. But he let himself down with further mistakes. His second was to say that he watched Little Bidding Irregulars almost every Saturday. But McCann had already been told that the Irregulars only ever play on Sundays.

3 Hargreaves said that the Barbadian player, Baz, was a fast bowler. McCann had been told that Baz was a batsman and a fielder, not a bowler at all. If Hargreaves was really a regular spectator, he would have known this.

4 Hargreaves claimed he often went behind the pavilion to retrieve cricket balls. But as McCann knew, there is a duck pond behind the pavilion, and any ball going over the pavilion was lost forever. Plainly Hargreaves was lying.

5 Hargreaves said that Little Bidding Irregulars were top of the league. But Bob had told McCann that the team did not play in a league. Again, Hargreaves was caught in a lie.

6 Hargreaves told McCann he was batting number eight. Obviously, then, he had seen the team list. But Mr Williams had told McCann that the team list was locked up in his suitcase with the Ashes. Hargreaves could not have seen the list unless he had broken into the suitcase and stolen the Ashes.

Useful information

The Royal Tournament
including the famous Field Gun Race every July at Earls Court.
Tel. 01-373 8141

RNLI Headquarters
West Quay Road, Poole, Dorset
BH15 1HZ

OXFAM Headquarters
274 Banbury Road, Oxford OX2 7DZ

The Kay Harker Books
The Midnight Folk/The Box of Delights by John Masefield published by Heinemann

John Masefield – A life by Constance Babbington-Smith, published by Oxford University Press (available in paperback, published by Hamish Hamilton, Nov. 1985).

Lee Boo – A Prince in Rotherhithe
published by Rotherside Books and available from Southwark Libraries, 20-22 Lordship Lane, London SE22 8HN

Matlock Cable Car
The Heights of Abraham, Matlock Bath, Derbyshire Tel. 0629 2365 Open 10.00-17.00 hrs (later in high season) price £1.50 for children, BUT Blue Peter Badge winners free of charge!

Kenya Tourist Office
13 New Burlington Street, London W1

Your Blue Peter badge now admits you to over 30 exhibitions and interesting places free of charge. If you'd like an up-to-date list, send a stamped addressed envelope to the Blue Peter Office, BBC TV Centre, London W12 7RJ.

Acknowledgements

Co-ordinator: **Gillian Farnsworth**

Designed by **Norman Brownsword** assisted by **David Tarbutt** and **Chris Rowell**

Masefield's Magic Box, The House Where Time Stood Still, and *Lee Boo* were written by **Dorothy Smith**

The Story of Dolly Shepherd was retold by Dorothy Smith from the book *When the 'Chute Went Up* by Dolly Shepherd with Peter Hearn and Molly Sedgwick, published by Robert Hale

John Masefield's Box of Delights, and *Lee Boo,* were illustrated by **Robert Broomfield**

Glitter Stars and *Lunapedes* by **Margaret Parnell**

The Case of the Ashen-faced Aussie was written by **Simon Barnes**

Other illustrations by Selwyn Hutchinson, Vernon Goodwin, Richard Geiger, Alan Burton and John Gilkes

Photographs were taken by Barry Boxall, David Clarke, Robert Hill, Michael Turner, John Ridley and Alex Leger, OXFAM with the exception of black & white photographs pp18-21 by permission of Walt Disney Pictures; Dolly Shepherd photographs pp24-26 by permission of Molly Sedgwick; White City Exhibition, Flip Flap and Dorando Pietri pp30-32 by BBC Hulton Picture Library; Football p31 by Press Sports Agency; Masefield aged 3 p38 by permission of Pamela Hugh-Jones, Schoolroom p39 by permission of Max Hamilton, Masefield with sister p39 by permission of Hiliary Magnus, Gilcruix by National Maritime Museum, Waterfront p39 by The Bettmann Archive, Inc; Pelican p51 by Ardea London; Red-billed hornbill p51 by Barnaby's Picture Library; Elephant p53 by Ian Brames, Ardea London; Lion p53 by Barnaby's Picture Library;
Lee Boo engraving p64 by permission of John Harvard Library.

BLUE PETER
COMPETITION

Would you like to come to TV Centre and meet Simon, Janet, Michael, Jack and Goldie? This could be your chance to come to London and meet them all at a special party – and see the Blue Peter studio!

Dethick Dilemma

James Mack and Andrea Lees were the two Top Prize winners in our Blue Peter End Papers Competition. You can see their designs at the beginning and the end of this book. We chose James's idea for the competition in our 22nd book and here it is:

How many animals are there on Simon's Dad's Farm?

There's more to this than meets the eye when you think that as well as sheep there are cows, goats, ducks, hens and dogs ...!
Only Simon's Dad knows the exact answer, and the 24 people who come up with the nearest number will be invited to our

James Mack

★ BLUE PETER ★ ★ PARTY ★

and there'll be lots of competition badges for the runners-up, too!

Write your answer on the entry form and send it to:
**Blue Peter
Dethick Dilemma Competition
BBC TV Centre
London W12 7RJ**

The closing date for entries is 13 January 1986.

First Prize Winners and runners-up will be notified by letter.

Andrea Lees

There are _____ animals on Simon's Dad's farm.

Name _____
Address _____
Age _____

This prize-winning picture was drawn by 6-year-old James Mack